The Authorities

Powerful Wisdom from Leaders in the Field

DEREK G. CHAN

Award Winning Author

ISBN - 978-1-77277-236-4

Limits of Liability and Disclaimer of Warranty
The author and publisher shall not be liable for your misuse of the enclosed material. This book is strictly for informational and educational purposes.

Warning – Disclaimer
The purpose of this book is to educate and entertain. The author and/or publisher do not guarantee that anyone following these techniques, suggestions, tips, ideas, or strategies will become successful. The author and/or publisher shall have neither liability nor responsibility to anyone with respect to any loss or damage caused, or alleged to be caused, directly or indirectly by the information contained in this book.

Medical Disclaimer
The medical or health information in this book is provided as an information resource only, and is not to be used or relied on for any diagnostic or treatment purposes. This information is not intended to be patient education, does not create any patient-physician relationship, and should not be used as a substitute for professional diagnosis and treatment.

Publisher
Authorities Press
Markham, ON
Canada

Printed in the United States and Canada.

FOREWORD

Experts are to be admired for their knowledge, but they often remain unrecognized by the general public because they save their information and insights for paying customers and clients. There are many experts in a given field, but their impact is limited to the handful of people with whom they work.

Unlike experts, authorities share their knowledge and expertise far more broadly, so they make a big impact on the world. Authorities become known and admired as leading experts and, as such, typically do very well economically and professionally. Most authorities are also mature enough to know that part of the joy of monetary success is the accompanying moral and spiritual obligation to give back.

Many people want to learn and work with well-respected and generous authorities, but don't always know where to find them. They may be known to their peers, or within a specific community, but have not had the opportunity to reach a wider audience. At one time, they might have submitted a proposal to the For Dummies or Chicken Soup for the Soul series of books, but it's now almost impossible to get accepted as a new author in such branded book series.

It is more than fitting that Raymond Aaron, an internationally known and respected authority in his own right, would be the one to recognize the need for a new venue in which authorities could share their considerable knowledge with readers everywhere. As the only author ever to be included in both of the book series mentioned above, Raymond has had the opportunity to give back and he understands how crucial it is for authorities to have a platform from which to share their expertise.

I have known and worked with Raymond for a number of years and consider him a valued friend and talented coach. He knows how to spot talented and knowledgeable people and he desires to see them prosper. Over the years, success coaching and speaking engagements around the world have made it possible for Raymond to meet many of these talented authorities. He recognizes and relates to their passion and enthusiasm for what they do, as well as their desire to share what they know. He tells me that's why he created this new nonfiction branded book series, The Authorities.

Dr. Nido Qubein

President, High Point University

TABLE OF CONTENTS

INTRODUCTION

This book introduces you to *The Authorities* — individuals who have distinguished themselves in life and in business. Authorities make a big impact on the world. Authorities are leaders in their chosen fields. Authorities typically do very well financially, and are evolved enough to know that part of the joy of monetary success is the accompanying social, moral and spiritual obligation to give back.

Authorities are not just outstanding. They are also *known* to be outstanding.

This additional element begins to explain the difference between two strategic business and life concepts — one that seems great, but isn't, and the other that fills in the essential missing gap of the first.

The first concept is "the expert."

What is an expert? The real definition is …

EXPERT: *a person who knows stuff*

People who have attained a very senior academic degree (like a PhD or an MD) definitely know stuff. People who read voraciously and retain what they read definitely know stuff. Unfortunately, just because you know stuff does not mean that anyone respects the fact that you do. Even though some experts are successful, alas, most are not — because knowing stuff is not enough.

Well, then, what is the missing piece?

What the expert lacks, "the authority" has. The authority both knows stuff and is *known* to know stuff. So, more simply …

AUTHORITY: *a person who is known as an expert*

The difference is not subtle. The difference is not merely semantic. The difference is enormous.

When it comes to this subject, there are actually three categories in which people fall:

- People who don't know much and are unsuccessful in life and in business. Most people fall in this category.
- People who know stuff, but still don't leave much of a footprint in the world. There are a lot of people like this.
- Experts who are also *known* as experts become authorities and authorities are always wondrously successful. Authorities are able to contribute more to humanity through both their chosen work and their giving back.

This book is about the highest category, *The Authorities* — people who have reached the peak in their field and are known as such.

You will definitely know some of *The Authorities* in this book, especially since there are some world-famous ones. Others are just as exceptional, but you may not yet know about them. Our featured author, Derek G. Chan, is one of these authors. Derek has been involved in Kung Fu since the young age of 8. He first started learning Wing Chun and Yang Style Tai Chi. After graduating from York university, Derek continued to develop his Kung Fu in the style of Wing Chun in Canada.

To take his experience and training to the next level, Derek next traveled to Hong Kong, the origin of Kung Fu cinema and the wellspring of Yip Man Wing Chun. During his stay, Derek continued his martial arts training where he further sharpened his skills and refine his techniques through the mentorship and guidance of various high-level grandmasters.

After returning from Hong Kong, Derek began training with a former special force military veteran. Through regular sparring sessions and military drills, Derek had the opportunity to further hone his martial arts techniques as they apply to real life combat and self-defence situations.

As an instructor, Derek hopes to help others by teaching them how to protect themselves practically and effectively through traditional Wing Chun forms and foundational skills, reinforced by techniques and skills applicable to real life combat and self-defence situations. He will also apply the holistic and wellness aspect of Wing Chun to individual's daily lives.

Aside from teaching martial arts and meditations, Derek is a certified personal trainer who specializes in performance training, as well a certified Life Coach. His goal is to help individuals achieve a higher level of mental and physical fitness.

They are *The Authorities*. Learn from them. Connect with them. Let them uplift you. Learning from them and working with them is the secret ingredient for success which may well allow you to rise to the level of Authority soon.

To be considered for inclusion in a subsequent edition of *The Authorities*, register to attend a future event at www.aaron.com/events where you will be interviewed and considered.

Unstoppable

The Art of Striving

DEREK G. CHAN

HOW TO BE UNSTOPPABLE

It has been said that in order to obtain a goal, one must first see it in the mind. The child who decides he wants a cookie from the jar that's high up on the shelf or the person who wants to make partner in the law firm where they now work—each uses the same mechanism or mindset. They understand at a visceral level that you become what you think about.

The difference between the student who can break boards with their hands and feet and the one who can't, isn't skill—it's all mindset, the belief, the deep-seated knowledge that one can do it.

Golf is an interesting game. The person who can best remember the components of a good swing AND can also envision them is the one who will hit the ball far, true and straight. So it is with martial arts: you must develop a set of beliefs or a mindset that will allow you to become unstoppable. Your approach needs to be holistic in nature.

Definition of Holistic: relating to or concerned with wholes or with complete systems rather than with the analysis of, treatment of, or dissection into parts

- Holistic medicine attempts to treat both the mind and the body
- Holistic ecology views humans and the environment as a single system

At Ko Fung Martial Art, we train body, mind and soul, integrating the three elements into a holistic mindset that will make you unstoppable in life.

One of my students, Lesia Rogers, had this to say about our "wellness" approach:

Sifu Derek has truly been a blessing to me, and I am extremely grateful. It has been a year this month since he took me under his wing to teach me how first to love myself. I've also been given many tools through martial art training, coaching and nutrition.

When I first started with Derek, I was already training with someone in Tai Chi, but I'd always wanted to learn self-defence and was looking for a different martial art. Interestingly, the first thing Derek coached me to do was slow down, something I still struggle with to this day.

In the beginning, I was extremely scared and hesitant, but Derek maintained a strong awareness and was always sensitive to my needs. This was important to me as I am an emotional person and needed to reset my mindset to love, acceptance, trust, building confidence and not being afraid of life. He spent hours with me and was by my side through the thick and thin of my life (my accomplishments and my challenges). It has not been an easy journey.

I learned that it takes time for change to happen, that it requires belief in ourselves, and through coaching and training Derek has given me the beautiful gift of awareness of who I really am and what I really want in life. He's made me realize anything is possible if I truly want it. For example, I spent five years with other trainers struggling with little change in my WEIGHT. The first thing Derek did was teach me about mindset to help me understand what it takes to achieve my weight loss goal. By slowing down, listening, AND DOING, I was able to lose 10 pounds in less than two months.

Most recently he has taught me that we often face challenges in life that we have no control over. With the sudden loss of my husband, he has taught me by being there for me that life must go on. In fact, if it wasn't for Derek in the past year, I wouldn't have been prepared to deal with this sudden loss and the corresponding changes in my life.

Change is very scary and can happen suddenly. Although nobody is ever really prepared for tragedy, we must move on and take back control of our lives. Derek has been very supportive and has taught me about acceptance, redirecting and letting go with everything we do in life.

I am a stronger person than I was a year ago when we first started. Thank you to Derek. I know I would be worse off without his coaching.

I had no idea how disciplined martial art can be until I met Derek and learned his way of life. And even though I am now alone (we are never really alone), I am beginning to fill the empty space within by learning to be by myself and love myself truly.

Grateful for every moment and every breath I take, thank you, Sifu Derek.

As mentioned, martial arts represent a pathway to developing a mindset that allows you to be unstoppable. I'll provide a holistic approach to developing this mindset in your own life and give you the tools to deal with hard times whenever you encounter them. You'll learn about martial arts principles and how to apply them to your daily living. Being unstoppable is not about fearlessness or strength, but about recognizing fear and still moving forward.

In training, a martial artist gets used to regular defeats and, in turn, sees them as an opportunity to learn. Tou Lou (martial art routine) or the forms in martial arts teaches us progression. One sequence of movements leads to another. You must learn each fundamental movement first before you can move to the next sequence of movements. This structured type of learning and milestone-based achievement is valuable in all aspects of life.

Wing Chun, in particular, is an effective tool to prepare those who practice it for real life. It does so by developing skills necessary for when one encounters difficult situations. Its concepts and principles are particularly enlightening when properly interpreted and digested under a good Sifu's guidance. Form in the Wing Chun system teaches the practitioner—Awareness, Body Structure, Balance, Body Mechanics and Relaxation. Technique drills or single drills in the Wing Chun system teach the individual how to use those principles during a confrontation.

An essential aspect of having an unstoppable mindset is the ability to make timely decisions in stressful and ambiguous situations. A decision may be either right or wrong, but it's crucial to remember that far worse than an incorrect decision is a situation where no decision is made when one is necessary. Through a variety of cooperative and semi-cooperative drills, a Wing Chun practitioner is able to develop intuition, reflexes and decision-making skills while under pressure.

An example of a Wing Chun drill that develops these skills is the famous 'Chi Sao' (sticking hand) training. It is a two-person tactile sensitivity drill. One only does the attacking while the other is only defending. The objective of the attacker is learning how to use leverage, distance, angle and openings to create a successful attack. At the same time, the defender is learning how to maintain proper body structure, relaxation and counter movements while under pressure with unplanned attacks. The key to Chi Sao is accepting the force coming in (relaxation) instead of using force against force.

This develops decision-making skills through checking assumptions against facts, and develops problem-solving skills by making its practitioners consider the possible impact of their decisions throughout the process of the drill. This gives the two practitioners an opportunity to test their strengths and weakness while promoting unique and unplanned learning processes to occur.

POWER OF BREATH - STRESS MANAGEMENT

A crucial concept in Wing Chun is that of proper breathing. Siu Nim Tao is the first open hand form from the Wing Chun system and is a form of breathing meditation. Siu Nim Tao translates to "Little Idea," meaning everything starts with a thought. Without proper breathing, movement becomes stilted and ineffective. Proper abdominal breathing is a skill that is crucial for a healthier and stronger body and also for focus, which is why it is one of the first things taught.

In addition to the health and training benefits of breathing, it can also be used as an important tool for stress management. Breathing has both voluntary and involuntary control mechanisms. You can shift from being its pilot to allowing it to be left on autopilot. The voluntary aspect of breathing is what allows us to tap into its stress-managing potential.

Breathing exercises act as a form of meditation in Chinese Martial Arts. Proper abdominal breathing used in this type of meditation allows a greater volume of breath and leads to a decrease in activity of stress markers and blood levels of stress hormones.

Oftentimes, when our life is stressed, the integrity of our automatic breathing suffers. Taking advantage of the control we can exert on breathing allows us to combat stress. Learning to control our breathing can allow us to begin to control other parts of our body as well. The mind-body connection developed through breathing exercises not only physically improves our breathing but can also increase self-awareness. When you bring your body and mind in tune, your mental state will be much improved, and less susceptible to stress.

BODY STRUCTURE

Martial arts teach the skills of how to use your body structure to your advantage, and offers understanding on how the body's structure works in terms of structural alignment, the linkage of the joints, and also how simple geometry and physics can be applied to the body. A central focus of Wing Chun is adopting particular stances and postures as a framework from which to launch attacks and counter-attacks. Doing this without good posture will greatly limit your ability to be effective. In fact, your Wing Chun techniques won't be as effective unless your body is aligned correctly. This alignment also reinforces the important concept of breathing and can directly impact your ability to draw and use your breath.

Good posture means that the body is aligned with gravity, walks tall and moves with freedom in the joints. Posture in martial arts is vitally important.

This is the reason most martial arts emphasize structure from the beginning. Physical structure from a Kung Fu point of view involves a little more than just good posture, though. In addition to good posture, it adds internal connections such that your entire body learns to move as a single fluid and powerful unit.

The efficient way to get a feel for a student's structure is through single drills, Chi Sao and sparring. Good structure can be almost invisible—even to the trained eye. However, the lack of it can usually be felt as soon as contact is made with your opponent. If an opponent has good structure, a lot of techniques you could try are unlikely to work, but if their structure is poor or non-existent, almost anything you do will be effective.

What exactly is good structure and why is it so important? To put it in simple terms, good structure is the way in which you connect the different parts of yourself together internally so that they are aligned with the forces acting on your body. In Wing Chun principle and theory, the curves of the spine should be aligned, eliminating as much curvature as much as possible. It's done by tucking in the chin backward and slightly scooping forward the tailbone to avoid an anterior pelvic title. Shoulders should be relaxed and dropping with the body. By doing so, the body is able to absorb and deliver a force as one bodily unit.

The majority of people are completely disconnected and don't have proper alignment and coordination with their body. Their arms will do one thing, their legs something different, with hips only being vaguely involved. When the body does so many different things, it's impossible to connect the breath or the mind to what it's doing. This results in internal chaos and a feeling that you lack the resources to cope with your physical situation. The truth is, you don't lack the resources at all; you've just scattered them. The key to good structure is in learning how to gather all the parts of yourself together so that you can put everything you are into everything you do.

Good structure connects your arms and legs together through your centre and involves your breath working in harmony with your movements. Most importantly, the whole process is controlled by your mind, which stays focused on what you're doing. When you're connected internally, every movement involves your whole body. This internal structure can easily be felt. For example, when you try to move someone's arm who is well connected internally, you can feel that in trying to move their arm you are moving the weight of their whole body.

RELAXATION

Relaxation is a great example taught in martial arts that can easily be applied to everyday life. To be relaxed is to be natural. It should be like pouring water into your cup without any muscle tension. To get a better understanding of how to apply this in daily life, we remember how relaxation, in the context of martial arts, is supposed to be understood.

When I teach Wing Chun, I like to begin by emphasizing to my students that, in training, techniques are performed in a relaxed manner. This occurs both during training and in actual combat. In order to develop force, one must be able to relax. Why? The equation for force is mass multiplied by acceleration, and if there's any sort of muscle tension, it will only slow down the acceleration. I tend to use an analogy of a car. In order for a car to move smoothly, you will have to step on the accelerator. Step on the brake and accelerator at the same time, and it will feel like you're getting a lot of power, but in reality, you're not going anywhere.

If the arm is tensed, maximum punching speed cannot be achieved. To begin a punching motion, the arm must, in essence, first be relaxed. If relaxed at the onset, the punching may begin at any time. It is a fact that one motion is always faster than two. If there is unnecessary tension, energy will be wasted, and this will, in turn, create fatigue. In an extended engagement, this can be critical. Tension stiffens your body and thus reduces your ability to sense and react to your opponent's intentions. Look at the sport of boxing. The best boxers don't get tired—even after 12 rounds. A huge part of this is that they don't waste energy on inefficient movement. Less experienced boxers may look good early in a fight, but they often crumble in the later rounds due to not being relaxed.

I will now paraphrase two of the core points of this lesson:

1. **Tense muscle slows down your reaction speed.**
2. **Unnecessary tension wastes energy, causing fatigue.**

If you're overcome by anger or are tense, your mind faces identical effects and, consequently, you'll have difficulty acting with the speed you need. This unnecessary tension in your mind doesn't only waste your energy and time, it also creates a lot of undesired situations that will now need to be solved. A person with a relaxed mind can always see things more clearly than a quick-tempered person. Thus, they can easily react with proper speed and attitude. This is why a person who understands the principle of relaxation correctly can certainly be more careful and successful; they react only when necessary by keeping calm and relaxed.

BALANCE

Balance is important to all martial arts, and especially Wing Chun. It's a concept that ties together both relaxation and structure. Without balance you can't maintain structure, nor can you be relaxed as you'll always be fighting to adjust yourself and the structure you've moved away from.

The Merriam-Webster dictionary defines balance as follows:

bal·ance noun \ba-lən(t)s

- The state of having your weight spread equally so that you do not fall
- The ability to move or to remain in a position without losing control or falling
- A state in which different things occur in equal or proper amounts or have an equal or proper amount of importance

Balance in Kung Fu is often associated with the physical sense of the word. I teach my students from the day they walk in how to understand their bodies in order to develop the balance necessary to perform the forms and techniques in Wing Chun. However, physical balance isn't the only form of balance a martial arts student should learn to hone. Balance in Wing Chun isn't only about your own physical body, but understanding how to create balance between two individuals. The highest level in the art of Wing Chun isn't about how to destroy or how to inflict the most pain in an individual, but how to neutralize and balance an opponent's incoming force without harming them, and at the same time preventing them from hurting you.

"The best battle is the one that has not been fought."

- Sun Tzu

This is one of the other reasons why in Wing Chun we'll focus heavily on Chi-Sao, as it helps us understand how to find balance between two individuals—either by changing to a different position or stepping in a different angle. This is one of the skills that's transferable to everyday life and relationship-building.

There is a saying that Wing Chun Kung Fu is easy to learn but hard to master. One reason is that, in the Wing Chun system, there's a fine balance between each movement and technique. Each movement needs to be precise. There can't be any gray area as it could be a matter of your life or death in a physical confrontation. In order to find the fine balance, though, one must understand not what to do but what not to do.

Understanding this concept will also help you find balance with your overall well-being and health. It's not about knowing what type of workout we should be doing or what type of food we should eat, but what we should not be doing or eating on a daily basis. Example: all rigorous physical activity can wear down the body, and you can feel tired, sore or injured. One must always balance training and rest, and in the case of an injury, you must listen to your body. Training when too fatigued or coming back too soon from an injury can set your training back by keeping you out even more in the long run.

ROOTING AND CENTRALIZATION

"When you have roots there is no reason to fear the wind."
- Chinese Proverb

In order to understand how to become unstoppable in classical martial arts training you must recognize that it all begins with the foundation. So what does the foundation include? Strengthening the lower body by lowering your center of gravity and widening up your base. Learning how to align your skeletal structure at the same time as relaxing your body. If we're able to be rooted to the ground and our body is up straight, it's most likely going to be harder to be pushed out of balance. You can try this when you are taking the bus or subway.

1. **Imagine your head is being slightly pulled up.**
2. **Widen your base (knees are a shoulder width apart).**
3. **Slightly bend your knees to lower your center of gravity.**

You'll automatically feel more balanced and centered. A solid base is required in order for you to grow your skills and techniques. It's the same in life. It's important to understand what keeps you grounded, to discover both your values and your beliefs. By doing so, you're able to hold your ground no matter what conditions life gives you.

By being grounded, you'll eliminate fear and find inner peace. This happens as you gain the courage and strength to overcome whatever fears you might have. Training in the martial arts will always push you to your limits. It tests not only your physical strength but your mental strength as well. Know this: each time you're ready to give up, you're facing a true test of willpower. You push yourself to the limit to see how much more you can take and to see how much more you're willing to go through in order to achieve your goal. This mental strength develops into an unbreakable warrior spirit, giving you the courage to persevere through your darkest hours.

ACCEPTANCE AND LETTING GO

At a certain point in your training the ability to 'let go' becomes essential. The concept of letting go functions on two levels—physical and mental. To be able to truly let go, the physical, mental (includes emotional) aspects must function in unison.

Physically you learn to relax and release your muscles, tendons and ligaments. When you do this, it leads to the deepening of one's root and the ability to ground a powerful incoming force. In terms of meditation, this means relaxing as much as possible and 'trusting' the Earth to hold you up.

The emotional and mental aspects of 'letting go' are intertwined, meaning that emotions can trigger thought patterns, and certain thought patterns can trigger emotions. You should look for evenness and balance in your emotion. This is a non-reactive state rather than an absence of emotion per se. This emotional neutrality is like a placid lake that appears to be a mirror. In this state, it becomes possible to read a person's true emotional intention like an open book.

For the mind, you want, at first, a gentle calmness and a slowing of thought, but this eventually develops into what has been termed 'mind of no mind.' This mind of no mind is actually an optimal state for both the meditative aspect as well as the martial. For meditation, we can perceive and become aware of things without the mind's judgement. In martial arts, this 'mind of no mind' state is optimal for success in combat. When centered in such a state you are able to act or react at a speed that can be faster than the speed of thought!

Accepting and letting go are probably two of the hardest things to do. Whether it's a relationship, anger from an argument or simply past mistakes; instead of being stuck in the moment, accept the emotion and the situation with your arms wide open. Acknowledge, embrace and let go. Let go of emotions and situations that don't serve you as a whole or lead you to greater things. It's beyond whether you were right or wrong. It's about setting yourself free. It begins with the willingness to accept ourselves exactly as we are, right where we are, with no judgements or preconceived notions. For the martial element, you must go even further. Instead of fearing an opponent's attack, you must learn to welcome it. This is all a matter of lack of tension. Therefore, the stronger an attack, the more relaxed you must initially become to deal with it. This method is grounded in a Wing Chun principle that states, "Accept what comes, escort what leaves." By accepting the incoming force, it will enable you to reposition and let go of what's coming in at you.

Once this is accomplished you no longer react to circumstances as average people do. Instead, you find yourself centered and alert—ready to deal with a situation without having your natural adrenal reaction getting in the way. This is not only supremely useful in combat but also in your daily life.

MOVING FORWARD

"Your one-step back is your opponent's two-step forward."

–Derek G. Chan

One of the most important rules of Wing Chun is that you don't step back. It is structure that gives us the advantage over the larger opponent, and when we become our worst enemy by destroying our own structure, it's not too difficult to predict the outcome of a fight. While Wing Chun may have backward stepping and backward bracing, these footworks are not designed for you to initiate. In Wing Chun we always move forward; only when the force dictates it do we actually move backwards. Footwork in Wing Chun is always taking you forward. It might be in a direct straight line or at an angle, but it allows you to swallow up any space that opens up between you and an attacker, limiting their options and overwhelming them.

Some of the most skilful boxers are those that can deliver a knockout blow while going backwards. While this may be much to the appreciation of the crowd, Wing Chun has no time for any of this. The footwork drives you forward all the time. One of the most important rules I always remind my students of during our sparring sessions is to continue to move forward—mentally and physically. It's important to create opportunities either by footwork, by stepping in a different angle, or a follow-up technique. There may be times when it is best to be stationary and wait for the perfect timing and openings. However, if you are against a more experienced opponent, the only chance of you overcoming the situation is by closing the distance and creating the opening. If you don't, not only do you have a lesser chance of winning, you're also leaving yourself vulnerable as a stationary target.

By having the attitude of forward movement, it will greatly benefit you in your daily life. Life is your experienced and stronger opponent. It doesn't matter how organized or how well-planned you are; life will always throw obstacles at you. In order for you to conquer them, you must start by moving forward. If you keep waiting for the perfect time or the perfect day, you'll never get anything done, and, sadly, you'll also miss a lot of opportunities. Instead, start moving forward and create your own path, regardless of how tough the situation is. If there's a will there is a way.

FOCUS

It can take a continuous daily effort to reach your goals. However, focusing on your long-term expectations, you'll find the strength to keep going even in the face of temporary setbacks. Those trained in Wing Chun will tell you that in the process you'll face a lot of challenges and setbacks. The students who are able to recognize that such setbacks are necessary hurdles and pitfalls they must navigate along the path to their destination are also the ones who succeed. Without that realization a student faces great difficulty overcoming those setbacks because they may lose sight of their long-term goals and allow themselves to get lost, joining the many casualties who fall by the wayside.

To focus, you must not only find a goal but also envision and look beyond at what lies ahead. The same principle applies to Karate practitioners when they attempt to break boards. If they only focus on the surface, their success rate of breaking the boards decreases as their force will be slowed down before they reach the target. However, if they are envisioning and telling themselves to hit behind or through the boards, the chance of them breaking the board is a lot higher.

Life is a series of experiences. There will be times where you're stuck in the moment. Whether it's a failure in a business partnership or the loss of a family member, it's up to you to endure and envision what lies ahead and continue to march forward. By doing so, you'll develop a stronger self and character. This is what separates those who are short-sighted from those who are long-sighted.

TECHNIQUE—EFFICIENT AND ECONOMICAL

"Offence is Defence, Defence is Offence."
- Wing Chun Proverb

One of Wing Chun's unique points is that it doesn't rely on any brute strength to overcome an adversary. We'll always place ourselves as the fragile person. Why? There will always be someone bigger, stronger and faster. And the way to overcome a larger assailant is by understanding the power of proper body structure and relaxation.

To become more efficient and economical with your movements, you'll defend and attack simultaneously. Doing so will allow you to become more efficient with your movements. One example is the Lap Da or Lap Sao technique. This is a technique where one hand sinks the opponent's straight attack while your other hand punches. In order to execute these fine movements, there will be an emphasis on body coordination drills. Without being coordinated, you wouldn't have the ability to execute the technique as smoothly. Wing Chun techniques often require you to have your hands and lower body cooperating with one another. Being well coordinated also means one is well-balanced. As human beings, we already apply the principle of balance while we are walking, our left hand will swing out, right foot steps forward, and vice versa. However, as a martial artist sometimes we tend to forget about this basic principle, and we think martial arts movements and everyday movements are two separate entities.

Having the Wing Chun mindset of being efficient will change our approach to handling daily tasks. It will help us realize how important it is to utilize our energy more efficiently (as it will help us manage time). In Wing Chun philosophy, time is an important factor. For this reason, each movement and technique has to be precise. As it could be a matter of life or death if you're in a confrontation. Every inch, every angle, every movement comes into play. Wing Chun is a system that does not discriminate, as it is not about who is bigger, stronger and faster. It's about understanding how to utilize proper body mechanics and physics to your advantage. It's understanding how to execute the most impactful thing efficiently and effectively in the limited time and energy you're given. This is why, in classical martial arts, you'll strike on vital spots and soft tissues on the opponent when placed in a life or death situation. By embracing this Wing Chun concept, you're able to focus more and utilize your time and energy more efficiently and effectively in your regular daily routine.

To learn more about Derek's method of Wing Chun visit us at
www.kofung.ca or contact us at info@kofung.ca

Step Into Greatness

LES BROWN

You have greatness within you. You can do more than you could ever imagine. The problem most people have is that they set a goal and then ask "how can I do it? I don't have the necessary skills or education or experience".

I know what that's like. I wasted 14 years on asking myself how I could be a motivational speaker. My mind focused on the negative—on the things that were in my way, rather than on the things that were not.

It's not what you don't have but what you think you need that keeps you from getting what you want from life. But, when the dream is big enough, the obstacles don't matter. You'll get there if you stay the course. Nothing can stop you but death itself.

Think about that last statement for a minute. There's nothing on this earth that can stop you from achieving what it is that you want. So, get out of your way, and quit sabotaging your dreams. Do everything in your power to make them happen—because you cannot fail!

They say the best way to die is with your loved ones gathered around your bed. But what if you were dying and it was the ideas you never acted upon, the gifts you never used and the dreams you never pursued, that were circled around your bed? Answer that question right now. Write down your answers. If you die this very moment what ideas, what gifts, what dreams will die with you?

Then say: I refuse to die an unlived life! You beat out 40 million sperm to get here, and you'll never have to face such odds again. Walk through the field of life and leave a trail behind.

One day, one of my rich friends brought my mother a new pair of shoes for me. Now, even though we weren't well off, I didn't want them; they were a size nine and I was a size nine and a half. My mother didn't listen and told my sister to go get some Vaseline, which she rubbed all over my feet. Then my mother had me put those shoes on, minding that I didn't scrunch down the heel. She had my sister run some water in the bathtub, and I was told to get in and walk around in the water. I said that my feet hurt. She just ignored me and asked about my day at school, how everything went and did I get into any fights? I knew what she was up to, that she was trying to distract me, so I said I had only gotten into three fights. After a while mother asked me if my feet still hurt. I admitted that the pain had indeed lessened. She kept me walking in that tub until I had a brand new pair of comfortable, size nine and a half shoes.

You see, once the leather in the shoes got wet, they stretched! And what you need to do is stretch a little. I believe that most people don't set high goals and miss them, but rather, they set lower goals and hit them and then they stay there, stuck on the side of the highway of life. When you're pursuing your greatness, you don't know what your limitations are, and you need to act like you don't have any. If you shoot for the moon and miss, you'll still be in the stars.

You also need coaching (a mentor). Why? There are times you, too, will find yourself parked on the side of the highway of life with no gas in the vehicle. What you need then is someone to stop and offer to pick up some gas down the road a ways and bring it back to you. That person is your coach. Yes, they are there for advice, but their main job is to help you through the difficulties that life throws at all of us.

Another reason for having a coach is that you can't see the picture when you're in the frame. In other words, he or she can often see where you are with a clarity and focus that's unavailable to you. They're not going to leave you parked along the road of life, nor are they going to allow you to be stuck in the moment like a photo in a frame.

And let's say you just can't see you're way forward. You don't believe it's possible. Sometimes you just have to believe in someone's belief in you. This could be your coach, a loved one or even a staunch friend. You need to hear them say you can do it, time and again. Because, after all, faith comes from hearing and hearing and hearing.

Look at it this way. Most people fail because of possibility blindness. They can't see what lies before them. There are always possibilities. Because of this, your dream is possible. You may fail often. In fact, I want you to say this: I will fail my way to success. Here is why.

I had a TV show that failed. I felt I had to go back to public speaking. I had failed, so I parked my car for ten years. Then I saw Dr. Wayne Dyer was still on PBS and I decided to call them. They said they would love to work with me and asked where I had been. I wasn't as good as I had been ten years before, as I was out of practice, but I still had to get back in the game. I was determined to drive on empty.

Listen to recordings, go to seminars, challenge yourself, and you'll begin to step into your greatness, you'll begin to fill yourself with the energy you need to climb to ever greater heights. Most people never attend a seminar. They won't invest money in books or audio programs. You put yourself in the top 5 percent just by making a different choice than the average person. This is called contrary thinking. It's a concept taken from the financial industry. One considers choosing the exact opposite behaviour of the average person as a way to get better than average results. You don't have to make the contrarian choice, but if you don't have anything to lose by going that road, why not consider the option?

Make your move before you're ready. Walk by faith not by sight and make sure you're happy doing it. If you can't be happy, what else is there? Helen Keller said, "Life is short, eat the dessert first."

What is faith? Many of us think of God when we think of faith. A different viewpoint claims that faith is a firm belief in something for which there is no proof. I would rather think of faith as something that is believed especially with strong conviction. It is this last definition I am referring to when I say walk by faith not by sight. Be happy and go forth with strong conviction that you are destined for greatness.

An important step on your way to greatness is to take the time to detoxify. You've got to look at the people in your life. What are they doing for you? Are they setting a pace that you can follow? If not, whose pace have you adjusted to? If you're the smartest in your group, find a new group.

Are the people in your life pulling you down or lifting you up? You know what to do, right? Banish the negative and stay with the positive; it's that simple. Dr. Norman Vincent Peale once said (when I was in the audience), "You are special. You have greatness within you, and you can do more than you could ever possibly imagine."

He overrode the inner conversations in my mind and reached the heart of me. He set me on fire. This is yet another reason for seeking out the help of a coach or mentor or other new people in your life. They can do what Dr. Peale did for me. They can set your passion free.

How important is it to have the right kind of person/people on your side? There was a study done that determined it takes 16 people saying you can do something to overcome one person who says you can't do something. That's right, one negative, unsupportive person can wipe out the work of 16 other supportive people. The message can't be any clearer than that.

Let's face the cold, hard truth: most people stay in park along the highway of life. They never feel the passion, the love for their fellow man, or for the work they do. They are stuck in the proverbial rut. What's the reason? There are many reasons, but only one common factor: fear — fear of change, fear of failure, fear of success, fear they may not be good enough, fear of competition, even fear of rejection.

"Rejection is a myth," says Jack Canfield, co-author of The Chicken Soup for the Soul series. "It's not like you get a slap in the face each time you are rejected." Why not take every "no" you receive as a vitamin, and every time you take one know you are another step closer to success.

You will win if you don't quit. Even a broken clock is right twice a day.

Professional baseball players, on average, get on base just three times out of every ten times they face the opposing pitcher. Even superstars fail half of the time they appear at the plate.

Top commissioned salespeople face similar odds. They make may make one sale from every three people they see, but it will have taken them between 75 and 100 telephone calls to make the 15 appointments they need to close their five sales for the week. And these are statistics for the elite. Most salespeople never reach these kinds of numbers.

People don't spend their lives working for just one company anymore. This means you must build up a set of skills and experiences that are portable. This can be done a number of ways, but my favourite approaches follow.

You must be willing to do the things others won't do in order to have tomorrow the things that others don't have. Provide more service than you get paid for. Set some high standards for yourself.

Begin each day with your most difficult task. The rest of the day will seem more enjoyable and a whole lot easier.

Someone needs help with a problem? Be the solution to that problem.

Also, find those tasks that are being consistently ignored and do them. You'll be surprised by the results. An acquaintance of mine used this approach at a number of entry-level positions and each time he quickly ended up being offered a position in management.

You must increase your energy. Kick it up a notch. We are spirits having a physical existence; let your spirit shine. Quit frittering away your energy. Use it to move you closer to the achievement of your dreams. Refuse to spend it on non-productive activities.

What do people say about you when you leave a room? Are you willing to take responsibility—to walk your talk. There is a terrible epidemic sweeping our nation, and it is the refusal to take responsibility for one's actions. Consider that at some point in any situation there will have been a moment where you could have done something to change the outcome. To that end you are responsible for what happened. It's a hard thing to accept, but it's true.

Life's hard. It was hard when I was told I had cancer. I had sunken into despair, and was hiding away in my study when my son came in. My son asked me if I was going to die. What could I do? I told him I was going to fight, even though I was scared. I also told him that I needed some help. Not because I was weak but because I wanted to stay strong. Keep asking until you get help. Don't stop until you get it.

A setback is the setup for a comeback. A setback is simply a misstep on the long road of success. It means nothing in the larger scheme of things. And, surprisingly, it sets you up for your next win. It tends to focus you and your energy on your immediate goals, paving the way for your next sprint, for your comeback.

It's worth it. Your dreams are worth the sacrifices you'll have to make to achieve them. Find five reasons that will make your dreams worth it for you. Say to yourself, I refuse to live an unlived life.

If you are casual about your dreams, you'll end up a casualty. You must be passionate about your dreams, living and breathing them throughout your days. You've got to be hungry! People who are hungry refuse to take no for an answer. Make NO your vitamin. Be unstoppable. Be hungry.

Let me give you an example of what I mean by hungry ...

I decided I wanted to become a disc jockey, so I went down to the local radio station and asked the manager, Mr. Milton "Butterball" Smith, if he had a job available for a disc jockey. He said he did not. The next day I went back, and Mr. Smith asked "Weren't you here yesterday?" I explained that I was just checking to see if anyone was sick or had died. He responded by telling me not to come back again. Day three, I went back again—with the same story. Mr. Smith told me to get out of there. I came back the fourth day and gave Mr. Smith my story one more time. He was so beside himself that he told me to get him a cup of coffee. I said, "Yes, sir!" That's how I became the errand boy.

While working as an errand boy at the station, I took every opportunity to hang out with the deejays and to observe them working. After I had taught myself how to run the control room, it was just a matter of biding my time.

Then one day an opportunity presented itself. One of the disc jockeys by the name of Rockin' Roger was drinking heavily while he was on the air. It was a Saturday afternoon. And there I was, the only one there.

I watched him through the control-room window. I walked back and forth in front of that window like a cat watching a mouse, saying "Drink, Rock, Drink!" I was young. I was ready. And I was hungry.

Pretty soon, the phone rang. It was the station manager. He said, "Les, this is Mr. Klein."

I said, "Yes, I know."

He said, "Rock can't finish his program."

I said, "Yes sir, I know."

He said, "Would you call one of the other disc jockeys to fill in?"

I said, "Yes sir, I sure will, sir."

And when he hung up, I said, "Now he must think I'm crazy." I called up my mama and my girlfriend, Cassandra, and I told them, "Ya'll go out on the front porch and turn up the radio, I'M ABOUT TO COME ON THE AIR!"

I waited 15 or 20 minutes and called the station manager back. I said, "Mr. Klein, I can't find NOBODY!"

He said, "Young boy, do you know how to work the controls?"

I said, "Yes, sir."

He said, "Go in there, but don't say anything. Hear me?"

I said, "Yes, sir."

I couldn't wait to get old Rock out of the way. I went in there, took my seat behind that turntable, flipped on the microphone and let 'er rip.

"Look out, this is me, LB., triple P. Les Brown your platter-playin' papa. There were none before me and there will be none after me, therefore that makes me the one and only. Young and single and love to mingle, certified, bona fide and indubitably qualified to bring you satisfaction and a whole lot of action. Look out baby, I'm your LOVE man."

I WAS HUNGRY!

During my adult life I've been a deejay, a radio station manager, a Democrat in the Ohio Legislature, a minister, a TV personality, an author and a public speaker, but I've always looked after what I valued most—my mother. What I want for her is one of my dreams, one of my goals.

My life has been a true testament to the power of positive thinking and the infinite human potential. I was born in an abandoned building on a floor in Liberty City, a low-income section of Miami, Florida, and adopted at six weeks of age by Mrs. Mamie Brown, a 38-year-old single woman, cafeteria cook and domestic worker. She had very little education or financial means, but a very big heart and the desire to care for myself and my twin brother. I call myself Mrs. Mamie Brown's Baby Boy and I say that all that I am and all that I ever hoped to be, I owe to my mother.

My determination and persistence in searching for ways to help my mother overcome poverty and developing my philosophy to do whatever it takes to achieve success led me to become a distinguished authority on harnessing human potential and success. That philosophy is best expressed by the following ...

"If you want a thing bad enough to go out and fight for it,
to work day and night for it,
to give up your time, your peace and your sleep for it...
if all that you dream and scheme is about it,
and life seems useless and worthless without it...
if you gladly sweat for it and fret for it and plan for it
and lose all your terror of the opposition for it...
if you simply go after that thing you want
with all of your capacity, strength and sagacity,
faith, hope and confidence and stern pertinacity...
if neither cold, poverty, famine, nor gout,
sickness nor pain, of body and brain,
can keep you away from the thing that you want...
if dogged and grim you beseech and beset it,
with the help of God, you will get it!"

Branding Small Business

RAYMOND AARON

Branding is an incredibly important tool for creating and building your business. Large companies have been benefiting from branding ever since people first started selling things to other people. Branding made those businesses big.

If you're a small business owner, you probably imagine that small companies are different and don't need branding as much as large companies do. Not true. The truth is small businesses need branding just as much, if not more, than large companies.

Perhaps you've thought about branding, but assumed you'd need millions of dollars to do it properly, or that branding is just the same thing as marketing. Nothing could be further from the truth.

Marketing is the engine of your company's success. Branding is the fuel in that engine.

In the old days, salespeople were a big part of the selling process. They recommended one product over another and laid out the reasons why it was better. Salespeople had credibility because they knew about all the products, and customers often took the advice they had to offer.

Today, consumers control the buying process. They shop in big box stores, super-sized supermarkets, and over the Internet — where there are no salespeople. Buyers now get online and gather information beforehand. They learn about all the products available and look to see if there really is any difference between them. Consumers also read reviews and check social media to see if both the company and the product are reputable. In other words, they want to know what the brand is all about.

The way of commerce used to be: "Nothing happens till something is sold." Today it's: "Nothing happens till something is branded!"

DEFINING A BRAND

A brand is a proper name that stands for something. It lives in the consumer's mind, has positive or negative characteristics, and invokes a feeling or an image. In short, it's a person's perception of a product or a company.

When all goes well, consumers associate the same characteristics with a brand that the company talks about in its advertising, public relations, marketing and sales materials. Of course, when a product doesn't live up to what the company says about it, the brand gets a bad reputation. On the other hand, if a product or service over-delivers on the promises made, the brand can become a superstar.

RECOGNIZING BRANDING AND ITS CHARACTERISTICS

Branding is the science and art of making something that isn't unique, unique. Branding in the marketplace is the same as branding on a ranch. On a ranch, ranchers use branding to differentiate their cattle from every other rancher's cattle (because all cattle look pretty much the same). In the marketplace, branding is what makes a product stand out in a crowd of similar products. The right branding gets you noticed, remembered and sold — or perhaps I should say bought, because today it is all about buying, not selling.

There are four main characteristics of branding that make it an integral part of the marketing and purchasing process.

1. Branding makes you trustworthy and known

Branding makes a product more special than other products. With branding, a normal, everyday product has a personality, and a first and last name, and people know who you are.

In today's marketplace, most products are, more or less, just like their competition. Toilet paper is toilet paper, milk is milk, and a grocery store by any other name is still a grocery store. However, branding takes a product and makes it unique. For example, high-quality drinking water is available from just about every tap in the Western world and it's free, but people pay good money for it when it comes in a bottle. Branding takes bottled water and makes Evian.

Furthermore, every aspect of your brand gives potential customers a feeling or comfort level that they associate with you. The more powerful and positive that feeling is, the more easily and more frequently they will want to do business with you and, indeed, will do business with you.

2. Branding differentiates you from others

Strong branding makes you better than your competition, and makes your product name memorable and easy to remember. Even if your product is absolutely the same as every other product like it, branding makes it special. Branding makes it the first product a consumer thinks about when deciding to make a purchase.

Branding also makes a product seem popular. Everyone knows about it, which implicitly says people like it. And, if people like it, it must be good.

3. Branding makes you worth more money

The stronger your branding is, the more likely people are willing to spend that little bit extra because they believe you, your product, your service, or your business are worth it. They may say they won't, but they will. They do it all the time.

For example, a one-pound box of Godiva chocolates costs about $40; the same weight of Hershey's Kisses costs about $4. The quality of the chocolate isn't ten times greater. The reason people buy Godiva is that the brand Godiva means "gift" whereas the brand Hershey means "snack". Gifts obviously cost more than snacks.

4. Branding pre-sells your product

In the buying age, people most often make the decision on which products to pick up before they walk into the store. The stronger the branding, the more likely people are to think in terms of your product rather than the product category. For example, people are as likely, maybe even more likely, to add Hellmann's to the shopping list as they are to write down simply mayo. The same is true for soda, ketchup, and many other products with successful, strong branding.

Plus, as soon as a shopper gets to the shelf, branding can provide a quick reminder of what products to grab in a few ways:

- An icon or logo
- A specific color
- An audio icon

BRANDING IN A SMALL BUSINESS

Big companies spend millions of dollars on advertising, marketing, and public relations (PR) to build recognition of a new product name. They get their selling messages out to the public using television, radio, magazines, and the Internet. They can even throw money at damage control when necessary. The strategies for branding are the same in a small business, but the scale, costs, and a few of the tactics change.

Make your brand name work harder

The name of a small business can mean everything in terms of branding. Your brand name needs to work harder for your business than you do. It's the first thing a prospective customer sees, and it is how they will remember you. A brand name has to be memorable when spoken, and focused in its meaning. If the name doesn't represent what consumers believe about a product and the company that makes it, then that brand will fail.

In building your product's reputation and image, less is often significantly more. Make sure the name you choose immediately gives a sense of what you do.

Large corporations have millions of dollars to take a meaningless brand name and make it stand for something. Small businesses don't, so use words that really mean something. Strive for something interesting and be right on point. You don't need to be boring.

Plumbers, for example, would do well setting themselves apart with names like "The On-Time Plumber" or "24/7 Plumbing". The same is true for electricians, IT providers, or even marketing consultants. Plenty of other types of business are so general in nature they just don't work hard enough in a business or product name.

Even the playing field: The Net

The Internet has leveled the playing field for small businesses like nothing else. You can use the Internet in several ways to market your brand:

Website: Developing and maintaining a website is easier than ever. Anyone can find your business regardless of its size.

Social Media: Facebook and Twitter can promote your brand in a cost-effective manner.

BUILDING YOUR BRAND WITH THE BRANDING LADDER

Even if you do everything perfectly the first time (and I don't know anyone who does), branding takes time. How much time isn't just up to you, but you can speed things along by understanding the different levels of branding, as well as the business and marketing strategies that can get you to the top.

Introducing the Branding Ladder

Moving through the levels of branding is like climbing a ladder to the top of the marketplace. The Branding Ladder has five distinct rungs and, unlike stairs, you can't take them two at a time. You have to take them in order, and some businesses spend more time on each rung than others.

You can also think of the Branding Ladder in terms of a scale from zero to ten. Everyone starts at zero. If you properly climb the ladder, you can end up at 12 out of 10. The Branding Ladder below shows a special rung at the top of the ladder that can take your business over the top. The following section explains the Branding Ladder and how your small business can move up it.

THE BRANDING LADDER	
Brand Advocacy	**12/10**
Brand Insistence	**10/10**
Brand Preference	**3/10**
Brand Awareness	**1/10**
Brand Absence	**0/10**

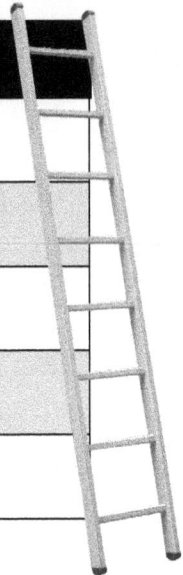

Rung 1: Living in the void

Your business, in fact every business, starts at the bottom rung, which is called brand absence, meaning you have no brand whatsoever except your own name. On a scale of one to ten, brand absence is, of course, zero. That's the worst place to live and obviously the most difficult entrepreneurially. The good news is that the only way is up.

Ninety-seven percent of businesses live on this rung of the Branding Ladder. They earn far less than they want to earn, far less than they should earn, and far less than they would earn if they did exactly the same work under a real brand.

Rung 2: Achieving awareness

Brand awareness is a good first step up the ladder to the second rung. Actually, it's really good, especially because 97 percent of businesses never get there. You want people to be aware of you. When person A speaks to person B and says, "Have you heard of "The 24/7 Plumber?" You want the answer to be "yes".

On that scale of one to ten, however, brand awareness is only a one. It's better than nothing, but not that much better. Although people know of your brand, being aware doesn't mean that they are interested in buying it. Coca Cola drinkers know about Pepsi, but they don't drink it.

Rung 3: Becoming the preferred brand

Getting to the third rung, brand preference, is definitely a real step up. This rung means that people prefer to use your product or service rather than that of your competition. They believe there is a real difference between you and others, and you're their first choice. This rung is a crucial branding stage for parity products, such as bottled water and breakfast cereals, not to mention plumbers, electricians, lawyers, and all the others. Brand preference is clearly better than brand awareness, but it's less than halfway up the ladder.

Car rental companies represent a perfect example of why brand preference may not be enough. When someone lands at an airport and needs to rent a car on the spot, he or she may go straight to the preferred rental counter. If that company has a car available, it's a sale. However, if all the cars for that company have been rented, the person will move to the next rental kiosk without much thought, because one rental car is just as good as another.

Exerting Brand Preference needs to be easy and convenient

If all you have is brand preference, your business is on shaky ground and you can lose business for the feeblest of reasons. Very few people go to a second or third supermarket just to find their favorite brand of bottled water. Similarly, a shopper may prefer one store over another but, if both stores sell the same products, he or she will often go to the closest store even if it is not the better liked one. The reason for staying nearby does not need to be a dramatic one — the shopper may simply be tired, on a tight schedule, or not in the mood to travel.

Rung 4: Making it you and only you

When your customers are so committed to your product or service that they won't accept a substitute, you have reached the fourth rung of the Branding Ladder. All companies strive to reach this place, called brand insistence.

Brand insistence means that someone's experience with a product in terms of performance, durability, customer service, and image has been sufficiently exceptional. As a result, the product has earned an incredible level of loyalty. If the product isn't available where the customer is, he or she will literally not buy something else. Rather, the person will look for the preferred product elsewhere. Can you imagine what a fabulous place this is for a company to be? Brand insistence is the best of the best, the perfect ten out of ten, the whole ball of wax.

Apple is a perfect example of brand insistence

Apple users don't just think, they know in their heads and hearts, that anything made by Apple is technologically-advanced, user-friendly, and just all-around superior. Committed to everything Apple, Mac users won't even entertain the thought that a PC may have positive attributes.

Apple people love everything about their Macs, iPads, iPhones, the Mac stores and all those apps. When the company introduces a new product, many of its brand-insistent fans actually wait in line overnight to be one of the first to have it. Steve Jobs is one of their idols.

Considering one big potential problem

Unfortunately, you can lose brand insistence much more quickly than you can achieve it. Brand-insistent customers have such high expectations that they can be disillusioned or disappointed by just one bad product experience. You also have to consistently reinforce the positives because insistence can fade over time. Even someone who has bought and re-bought a specific brand of car for the last 20 years can decide it's just time for a change. That's how fickle the world is.

At ten out of ten, brand insistence may seem like the top rung of the ladder, but it's not. One rung is actually better, and it involves getting your brand-insistent customers to keep polishing your brand for you.

Rung 5: Getting customers to do the work for you

Brand advocacy is the highest rung on the ladder. It's better than ten out of ten because you have customers who are so happy with your product that they want everyone to know about it and use it. Think of them as uber-fans. Not only do they recommend you to friends and family, they also practically shout your praises from the rooftops, interrupt conversations among strangers to give their opinion, and tell everyone they meet how fantastic you are. Most companies can only aspire to this level of customer satisfaction. Apple is one of the few large corporations in recent history that has brand advocates all over the world.

- Brand advocacy does the following five extraordinary things for your company. Brand advocacy:
- Provides a level of visibility that you couldn't pay for if you tried. Brand advocates are so enthusiastic they talk about you all the time, and reach people in ways general media and public relations can't. You get great visibility because they make sure people actually listen.
- Delivers free advertising and public relations. Companies love the extra super-positive messaging, all for free.
- Affords a level of credibility that literally can't be bought. Brand advocates are more than just walking testimonials. They are living proof that you are the best.
- Provides pre-sold prospective customers. Advocate recommendations carry so much weight that they are worth much more than plain referrals. They deliver customers ready and committed to purchasing your product or service.
- Increases profits exponentially. Brand advocates are money-making machines for your business because they increase sales and decrease marketing costs.

For these reasons, brand advocacy is 12 out of 10!!

BRANDING YOURSELF: HOW TO DO SO IN FOUR EASY WAYS

If you're interested in branding your product or company, you may not be sure where to begin. The good news: I'm here to help. You can brand in many ways, but here I pare it down to four ways to help you start:

Branding by association

This way involves hanging out with and being seen with people who are very much higher than you in your particular niche.

Branding by achievement

This way repurposes your previous achievements.

Branding by testimonial

This way makes use of the testimonials that you receive but have likely never used.

Branding by WOW

A WOW is the pleasantly unexpected, the equivalent of going the extra mile. The easiest and most certain way to WOW people is to tell them that you've written a book. To discover how you can write a book of own, go to www.BrandingSmallBusinessForDummies.com.

Sex, Love and Relationships

DR. JOHN GRAY

Just as great sex is important to lasting love, good health is important to sex and relationships. About 12 years ago, I cured myself of early stage Parkinson's disease. The doctors were amazed, but my wife was even more amazed. She noted that our relationship and sex life had become dramatically better. It turns out that the natural supplements I used to reverse Parkinson's can also make you more attentive and loving in your relationship. At that point, I realized that good relationship skills alone were not enough to sustain love and passion for a lifetime.

I shared many insights gained from my 40 years' experience as a marriage counselor and coach in *Men Are From Mars, Women Are From Venus*. And while my insights go a long way towards helping men and women understand and support each other, good communication skills alone are not always enough. For better relationships, we not only need to be healthy, but we must also experience optimum brain function.

If you are tired, depressed, anxious, not sleeping well, or in pain, then certainly romantic feelings will become a thing of the past. My recovery from Parkinson's revealed to me the profound connection between the quality of our health and our relationships. This insight has motivated me, over the past twelve years, to research the secrets of optimum health as a foundation for lasting love.

These are health secrets that are generally not explored in medical school. In medical school, doctors are indoctrinated into the culture of examining the symptoms, identifying the sickness, and prescribing a drug to treat that sickness. They learn very little about how to be healthy or to sustain successful relationships.

There are no university courses entitled "Better Nutrition For Better Sex". Drugs sometimes save lives, but they also have negative side effects that do little to preserve the passion in a relationship. Ideally, drugs should be used as a last resort and 90 % of our health plan should be drug free. From this perspective, the heath care crisis, as well as our high rate of divorce in America, is indirectly caused by our dependence on doctors and prescription drugs.

Most people have not even considered that taking prescribed drugs (even for the small stuff) can weaken their relationships, which in turn makes them more vulnerable to more disease. For example, if you are feeling depressed or anxious, a drug may numb your pain, but it does nothing to help you correct the cause of your problem. It can even prevent you from feeling your natural motivation to get the emotional support you need. In a variety of ways, our common health complaints are all expressions of two major conditions: our lack of education to identify and support unmet gender-specific emotional needs; and our lack of education to identify and support unmet gender-specific nutritional needs.

With an understanding of natural solutions that have been around for thousands of years, drugs are not needed to treat many common complaints. Some symptoms like low energy, weight gain, allergies, hormonal imbalance, mood swings, poor sleep, indigestion, lack of focus, ADD and ADHD, procrastination, low motivation, memory loss, decreased libido, PMS, vaginal dryness, muscle and joint pain, or the lack of passion in life and/or our relationships can be treated drug-free. By using drugs (even over-the-counter drugs) to treat these common complaints, our bodies and relationships are weakened, making us more vulnerable to bigger and more costly health challenges like cancer, diabetes, heart disease, auto-immune disease, dementia, and Alzheimer's. In simple terms, by handling the easy stuff (the common complaints) without doctors and drugs, we can protect ourselves from the big stuff (cancer, heart disease, dementia, etc.) We can be healthy and also enjoy lasting love and passion in our personal lives.

Even if you are taking anti-depressants or hormone replacement therapy, sometimes all it takes to stop treating the symptom is to directly handle the cause. With specific mineral orotates (something most people have never heard of) or omega three oil from the brains of salmon, your stress levels immediately drop and you begin to feel happy and in love again.

For every health challenge, we have explored the effects on our relationships, with as well as natural remedies that can sometimes produce immediate positive results. You can find these natural solutions to common health complaints for free at my website: www.MarsVenus.com.

What they don't teach in medical school is how to be healthy and happy without the use of drugs or hormone replacement. By refusing drugs and taking responsibility for your health, a wealth of new possibilities can become available to you. We are designed to be healthy and happy, and it is within our reach if we commit to increasing our knowledge.

New research regarding the brain differences in men and women reveals how specific nutritional supplements, combined with gender-specific relationship and self-nurturing skills, can stimulate the hormones of health, happiness and increased energy. Over the past 10 years in my healing center in California, I witnessed how natural solutions coupled with gender-specific relationship skills could solve our common health complaints without drugs. By addressing these common complaints without prescribed drugs, not only do we feel better, but our relationships have the potential to improve dramatically.

Ultimately the cause of all our common complaints is higher stress levels. Researchers around the world all agree that chronic stress levels in our bodies provide a basis for any and all disease to take hold. An easy and quick solution for lowering our stress reactions is specific nutritional support combined with gender-smart relationship skills. Extra nutritional support is needed because stress depletes the body very quickly of essential nutrients. When a car engine is running more quickly, it uses fuel more quickly. When we are stressed, we need both extra nutrients and extra emotional support. Understanding what we need to take and where to get it requires education. Every week day at www.MarsVenus.com I have a live daily show where I freely answer questions and provide this much-needed new gender-specific insight.

At www.MarsVenus.com, we are happy to share what we have learned for creating healthy bodies and positive relationships. You can find a host of natural solutions for common complaints and feel confident that you have the power to feel fully alive with an abundance of energy and positive feelings that will enrich all your relationships.

Investment Success and Successful Beliefs

JASON G. CHAN

"Why are you chuckling to yourself?" my brother asked as we passed by an upscale restaurant one night. "Did I miss something?"

"No, not really," I replied. "Remember those two Ferraris that were waiting for valet parking back by the restaurant that almost everybody who passed by, including us, were looking at and admiring? I just realized that if I wanted to, I could buy both of those Ferraris with cash, one for you and one for me."

Of course, I never did that. But that moment stuck in my head because it was the first time I realized that, financially, I had done okay for myself. I made my first million dollars investing in the stock market when I was just shy of 30 years old. My second million came shortly after that. That's when I stopped counting. I stopped counting because I finally found some comfort in knowing that my family was doing okay and that I was doing okay.

A few years before that, my father had suddenly passed away. It happened in 2008 in the middle of one of the greatest recessions in history. My family was entrenched in debt and my parents hardly had any retirement savings, let alone other investments. My two younger brothers and I were burdened knee-deep in student loan debt. I was living in my parents' living room because the basement where I had been living got flooded and became too moldy to stay in.

For most of my adolescent and early adult life, our family cash flow was tight, and we couldn't even afford a decent study desk. I haven't done too shabby for a boy whose desk was actually nothing more than a door flipped sideways and propped up by four poles on each corner; definitely not too shabby as an investor for someone whose degree was in fine arts and graphic design. I don't have a degree in business, finance or economics. I don't believe we need fancy degrees or education to do well in finance and investments or in life. For those who likes degrees, later in life I was told that I actually got a PhD earlier in life, since I was Poor, Hungry and Driven. At the end of the day, it's not your degrees or titles that make you, it's really about your vision and your beliefs.

YOUR BELIEFS ARE IMPORTANT

Sometimes people ask me what I did or what I invested in, hoping to get some insight as to how they too can achieve what I have. They're usually asking about specific things I did, specific things I invested in, or tools I used. What they don't understand is that these things are not the important part. Belief is where it all starts. To achieve investment success by having the proper successful beliefs, mental concepts, and proper mindset is the key.

After all, we all act and behave in certain ways because of our beliefs. Some beliefs serve us, some limit or deter us, and some set us astray. They shape what we do and how we do it. Before anything even starts, our beliefs tell us what we can do because they shape what we think is possible and what is not. Therefore, having the proper beliefs, or shaping what you already have, is really important in life, and also in investments. My purpose and goal is to help you adopt proper, empowering beliefs and realign, even discard, the negative ones as they relate to investments. It is only with a proper mindset and a successful beliefs system that you can get ahead in finances and achieve sustainable, consistent and long term investment success.

The first and, perhaps, the most important belief I want to share with you is it's possible for you to achieve financial and investment success. Not only can you achieve it, but you can achieve it on your own by empowering yourself to take control of your finances and investments. If a poor boy who started off living in a basement with a door as a study desk, who studied fine arts and graphic design, and who had large student loans and family debt could do it, so could you.

"It's Possible" is one of my favorite phrases from Les Brown. He goes on to describe that one of the keys to changing our belief system and enabling us to act on our dreams is knowing that something is possible. To know that a goal or that dream or that something we want or achieve has already been done or achieved by someone else, is to know that something is possible and achievable. More importantly, that "It's Possible" for you to achieve it too!

UNDERSTANDING FINANCE AND INVESTMENTS IS A LIFE SKILL

One of the first questions people come across when it comes to their finances and investments is, "Should I manage them myself or should I get someone else in the financial industry, such as an investment firm or bank, to manage them for me?"

Not only am I an individual investor who manages my own finances, I have also worked in the financial services industry, for one of the largest financial institutions in the country, as an investment sales representative for over 10 years. I am also a certified life coach who specializes in finance and investments. Through my various experiences, my short answer is that you should eventually invest in yourself and invest for yourself. Being able to take control and take charge of your finances and investments is a very liberating feeling that everyone should enjoy.

The investment service industry has a purpose and a place in everybody's life, but by no means should it be used or regarded as a long-term solution. It's like riding a bicycle with training wheels. Many people dream of financial freedom, but they are often dependent on an investment company to get them there. How could you be free and dependent at the same time?

Understanding finance and investments is a necessity in life. Just like eating and cooking, it's something we have to do for the rest of our lives. For this reason, I believe it's a life skill we should all acquire and develop. We have to deal with money, so we need to understand finance. Unless we spend every dime we earn or put everything under a mattress, we all have to invest. At the end of the day, nobody cares more about your financial future and well-being more than you.

HAVING SOMEONE ELSE MANAGE YOUR MONEY IS MORE COSTLY THAN YOU THINK

When it comes to eating, we won't eat out every meal, every day for the rest of our lives. We won't do that because we know it doesn't make sense and it gets expensive. So why would it make sense to pay someone else or a company to manage your investments every day for the rest of your life? Well, many people actually do that. One of the main reasons is because the investment industry has presented their fees in a way that seems deceivingly small and inexpensive. That's why many people don't mind "dining out" their whole lives.

Let's use the mutual fund industry as an example. The mutual fund industry is what most people are exposed to and familiar with when it comes to professional investment management. Aside from possible front-load and back-load fees and commissions, all mutual funds charge what they call a management expense ratio or MER. The MER alone for the average mutual fund ranges from approximately 2% - 2.5% a year. We'll take the low end of 2% to give them the benefit of the doubt. A 2% annual fee sounds small and nominal, doesn't it? The financial industry usually does not take the time or effort to explain what this fee actually means. Often customers are left with the impression that they get charged 2% MER from the gains that the company makes for them, if any.

In reality, that 2% MER is calculated and charged based on the entire amount of money they are managing for the customer, or what they call assets under management. What that means is, if you give them $100 to invest, they will charge you 2% on that $100, so essentially $2. Say you have $100,000 invested with them. At 2% MER, that works out to be $2,000 a year. For those who wish to have $1,000,000 ($1 Million dollars) a 2% MER would cost them $20,000 a year! To look at it from another perspective, a 2% MER fee in 5 years alone, works out to 10% (2% x 5). In 10 years, that works out to be 20% (2% x 10). In a mere 5 years and 10 years respectively, you would have paid out 10% and 20% of your hard-earned money in MER fees. Now consider that most people save and invest for retirement for about 35 years, how does the math work out for a long duration like that?

As I mentioned, the financial and investment industry is a business. Just like the restaurant industry and eating out, there is a time and place for services like that. However, it should not be used as a long-term solution, because it becomes very costly in the long run. I feel a true investment company and professional should be promoting financial freedom and independence, not financial dependence. Understanding finance and investments is truly a life skill that we should all acquire and develop. We can't afford not to.

In the examples above, I purposely kept the math simple and to the point and avoided financial jargon, such as compounding, time value, etc., because those are the kind of things that deter from the basic idea and confuse clients. The investment industry will critique our example and try to say that they will grow the client's money through the years. However, at the end of day, they cannot guarantee you any gains. So we won't factor that in. And to be fair, I won't assume they'll lose your money either. I kept it neutral in my example—no gains, no losses—similar to the "lost decade" that we experienced in the stock markets not too long ago.

INVESTING IS LIKE TREASURE HUNTING

When most people think of the world of investments and finance it seems overwhelmingly complex. A simple and interesting analogy I use to compare the world of investing and the investment industry is a big treasure hunt. If we were to look at it from this perspective, we would get a better understanding of how things work, many things would become apparent and begin to make sense.

So off to treasure hunting we go. Imagine we are in a world where treasure hunting is a big deal and almost everybody is out to find some treasure. Opinions on how to find treasure are a dime a dozen and everybody has their ideas and opinions.

Yet, despite the abundance of ideas and strategies floating around, many of these ideas tend to be passed around by people who have never found any significant treasure themselves. They hear and get these ideas and concepts from family members, a friend, a friend of a friend, and various media outlets. And where did many of these ideas originate from? A lot of these ideas actually came about through the "treasure hunting industry."

Yes, treasure hunting is such a big deal, there's actually a treasure hunting industry which is supposedly there to help you and guide you to find treasure. There are big corporate institutions with many employees who sell you treasure maps, treasure guides, strategies, tools and gadgets along with various products and services which they claim will help you find treasure. Many of them offer packaged plans to help treasure hunt for you through their professional and experienced treasure hunters.

The deal is that you put up all the capital to be used for the treasure hunt, but they do not guarantee you any success. The only guarantee is that they will charge you a management fee whether or not they find you treasure. And if they do end up finding treasure, they actually take a bigger cut of your money. So you put up all the money and take all the risk and they take a risk free payment from you in order to help you treasure hunt. And there are no guarantees of success. It's a pretty good business model for them, but not such a good business idea for you.

At some point you might begin to wonder that if these companies and their staff are so good at treasure hunting, how come they just don't focus on that and treasure hunt for themselves? Eventually, you'll realize that these companies actually make money from selling treasure hunting packages and products and by providing treasure hunting services. They don't make their money from actually finding treasure, per se.

Their frontline staff, sales representatives and professional treasure hunters, can give you all sorts of treasure hunting advice, ideas, and strategies, along with various treasure products and services the company has to offer. However, like most regular people, most of them have never found success in treasure hunting. The majority of their income actually comes from working their sales jobs and earning commission selling treasure hunting packages, products and services.

Sometimes you see some of these sales people enjoying the luxuries of life which can create the impression that they have actually found treasure from treasure hunting, but the reality is, they were actually just a successful sales person, not a successful treasure hunter.

Remember how we said that much of the common investment advice that floats around in public originated from these treasure hunting companies in the treasure hunting industry? A lot of the time this supposed treasure hunting advice is actually based on half-truths that are either outdated, have lost effectiveness, or have never been useful at all. They are mainly ideas and strategies used to promote and sell various treasure hunting packages, products and services.

There are actually really good and skillful treasure hunters out there. As you would expect, most of them spend their time treasure hunting for themselves. Some do open up treasure hunting companies to help others find treasure, but they usually require clients with lots of money and many of them have reached capacity and have stopped taking on new clients.

Keep this treasure hunting analogy in mind the next time you think about investments and the investment industry. It should give you an idea of how to make sense of it all and help you decide if you really wish to have someone else treasure hunt for you or not.

THE INVESTMENT LANDSCAPE HAS CHANGED

Since the new millennium, the stock market and investment landscape has been a lot different than it was in previous decades. This is not just a belief—it is a fact. It is important that we recognize and acknowledge this reality and incorporate it into our belief system for two main reasons.

First of all, in order to invest successfully and navigate through the stock market, we need to understand what kind of landscape and environment we are currently in. Imagine you are taking a road trip, how could you expect a to get from point A to point B if you were using an old and dated road map from many decades ago? I am sure it would be a frustrating trip with a few wrong turns here and there.

Secondly, understanding how the stock market and investment landscape used to be can help us understand where many investment ideas and strategies we still hear and read about came to be. More important is why they have lost relevance, effectiveness and significance.

Using the beginning of the new millennium, the year 2000, as a benchmark for the midpoint year of reference, let us take a look at the last 36 years of the S&P500, a popular and widely followed North American stock index. We will take a look and compare the 18 years prior to the new millennium and 18 years since the new millennium. So from 1982 to 2000, compared to 2000 to 2018.

In terms of returns, if you were to just buy and hold from the beginning of 1982 to the beginning of 2000, the 18 years prior to 2000, the total return of the S&P 500 was approximately 1,100%. From the beginning of 2000 to the beginning of 2018, the last 18 years, the total return of the S&P 500 was approximately 92%. A 1,110% return compared to a 92% return. That's a difference of almost 12 times.

In terms of declines and recovery, between 1982 and 2000, the two biggest drops were Black Monday of 1987, which saw an approximately 36% drop from top to bottom, which took 8 months to break even, and August of 1998 which saw an approximately 23% drop from top to bottom, which took less than 2 months to break even.

In terms of declines and recovery, between 2000 and 2018, the two biggest drops were an approximately 50% drop during the years from early 2000 to early 2003. If you happened to have bought at the peak, it would have taken you about 7.5 years to break even. Then an approximately 57% drop from mid 2007 to early 2009. If you happened to have bought at the peak, it would have taken you about 6 years to break even.

From 1982 to 2000, there was a 23% to 36% drop, with a recovery time of 2 to 8 months, compared to the years from 2000 to 2018, in which there was a 50% to 57% drop, with a recovery time of 6 to 7.5 years. From declines to recoveries, there was a dramatic difference in magnitude.

To summarize, it is important that we recognize and acknowledge that the investment landscape has changed a lot in the last 20 years because many investment strategies and ideologies we still hear today were developed during that comparatively stable and less volatile time. However, due to the changes we have seen in the last 20 years, many of these strategies and ideologies have lost their effectiveness, value, and relevance. The conclusion is, since our investment landscape has changed and evolved, we too need to evolve and adapt our investment strategies to the present. We cannot just keep on blindly using what has worked in the past.

WE INVEST IN OUR BELIEFS, NOT THE MARKETS

As we started off by mentioning, beliefs are very important when it comes to investing. They affect how we invest: if we take charge of our investments ourselves, have someone else invest for us or if we even invest at all. More importantly, I have to stress the importance of adopting the right and proper beliefs because ultimately when we are investing, we are investing in our beliefs. People often think they are investing in the markets, but actually what they are investing in is their beliefs about the markets. This is a critical concept to keep in mind. Personally, understanding and realizing that concept helped take my investments to the next level.

This reality might be a little difficult to wrap our heads around at first, but consider this, the markets behave the same for everyone. If we are just investing in the markets, we should all get similar if not identical results. But we don't. How come some people make more money than others in a rising market, for example? Or how come some are able to profit from a recession while others lose a fortune? The market's behaviour and performance does not vary from one person to another. It is the beliefs about the markets that vary from one person to another. Therefore, one of the main keys to being able to invest successfully is to have the proper beliefs in regards to investing and the markets.

GENUINE INVESTMENT ADVICE AND POOR INVESTMENT ADVICE

Many of our beliefs regarding investments have been acquired and shaped by various pieces of investment advice we've come across over time. And there's all sorts of investment concepts, strategies, and theories. Which ones serves us? Which ones do not? There was a time when it was tough getting information, let alone getting information in a timely manner. But today, with the evolution of technology via computers, smartphones and the internet, we live in a time of information overload. Investment ideas and strategies are a dime a dozen. Almost everyone seems to have an idea of what to do. We come across so many investment ideas and so much advice. Often, the more we learn the more confused we get, as many of these investment ideas seem to contradict each other. How do we organize and conceptualize them all in a context that makes sense? As an individual investor I, too, had to struggle with that problem.

After years of study, research and practical hands-on experience investing my own money, as well as working in the finance and investment sales industry, I was finally able to sort and put everything in context. This belief system is a mental construct meant to organize all the ideas, advice, theories, strategies, and concepts I've accumulated as they relate to investments. I'll just refer to all of that as "investment advice" for simplicity.

It's obvious there's some investment advice that works and some that does not. So, I separate them into two categories: "Genuine Investment Advice" and "Poor Investment Advice." Within those two categories, there are actually two sub-categories we could further separate the investment advice into.

Within Genuine Investment Advice, the first subcategory is investment advice that I believe is almost universal and works for almost everyone. For example, diversification, cutting losses short, letting winners grow, and waiting for favourable risk to return opportunities before investing.

The second subcategory, as well as all the other categories we'll touch upon, is where things get interesting. It's where it causes lots of confusion among people's belief systems and is a source of frustration for many. Within this second sub-category of Genuine Investment Advice is the investment advice that is accurate and works but may not work for everyone, because it depends on their personality and their investment style. For example, many investment ideas, theories, and strategies seem like complete opposites when you compare them with one another: value investing versus momentum investing, swing trading versus momentum investing, fundamental analysis versus technical analysis, short-term trading versus long-term investing, buy low and sell high versus buy high and sell higher, and top down versus bottom up investment styles. All these investment ideas and strategies work, but success depends on how they match the individual investor's personality and how they are used alongside their investment style. In a nutshell, those are examples of Genuine Investment Advice.

On the other end of the spectrum from Genuine Investment Advice we have Poor Investment Advice. It's basically advice that is not effective or does not work. Within this main category, it also has two sub-categories.

In the first sub-category is investment advice that used to work but is outdated because of the change in the investment landscape that we touched upon earlier. It used to work and perhaps even used to deliver great results but has since greatly lost value and effectiveness. Yet, these investment ideas still get passed around by many people because they have failed to recognize that the investment landscape has dramatically changed and evolved in recent years.

Some examples are: index investing, buying and holding indiscriminately, dollar cost averaging, and investing on a consistent and regular schedule regardless of overall market conditions. It's easy to see where such investment ideas, strategies and advice come from once we understand how the investment landscape used to be and what had happened in the past. Like we've seen in our example, the stock market, namely the S&P500, went up approximately 1,100% from 1982 to the year 2000. Yet, in our recent investment landscape from 2000 to the beginning of 2018, the total return of the S&P500 was a mere 92%—a return that's dramatically less than 1/12th in the same 18-year time span. That is less than 10% of the 1,100% return the we've seen from 1982 to the year 2000.

The second subcategory of Poor Investment Advice is the one which I despise the most. They are essentially "investment advice" that was never effective and never worked. For example, advice such as "If you don't sell your losing position, you aren't really losing money because unless you cash out, it's only a paper loss." That is as foolish as saying "If you go to the casino and convert your cash into casino chips, then you lose your chips, you're not actually losing money unless you convert those chips back into cash." Then there's "Adding to losses and losing positions is beneficial because when you average down, it gives you better value and a lower overall price point." With this strategy, you are not only not cutting your losses, you are adding to an already losing position. Technically, you could use this flawed logic to invest in a company as it goes all the way down to bankruptcy because it suggests the lower the price goes, the more you should invest. There is also "Focus on the long-term, and don't worry that your stocks are down because you're still getting paid dividends." Focusing solely on dividends presents a very distorted and partial picture, as you should be focusing on total return which consists of dividends plus any capital gains or losses. With that in mind, if your stock is down -40%, it would be foolish to say it's alright because you're receiving a 3% dividend yield.

People often ask, "If such investment advice doesn't work, then why do people say these things?" The answer is because these ideas mainly originate and get spread around by unscrupulous individuals in the financial and investment industry. In reality, such investment advice was merely conjured up to promote and sell investment products to customers and keep their customers invested so they could continue to charge them various fees and commissions.

Unfortunately, because much of this investment advice came from individuals within the financial and investment industry, it gave them a false sense of credibility and such bad advice got perpetually circulated. This is especially true because the advice is usually mixed in with some rationalization and half truths. When I say half truths, I am also referring to the dated investment advice that we mentioned earlier. I consider those half truths, because those strategies used to work, but have greatly lost significance since. Nevertheless, such bad advice is still often used as sales pitches by individuals in the industry to promote and sell various investment products.

Notice that all such advice falls under a similar underlying idea. It is to tell the customer that it is always a good time to invest and once they are invested, to never sell. For example, when the markets are high, they will say you should invest more because things are going well and you are making money. When the markets are low, they will say you should invest more because you are getting good value. Also, it is always a good time to invest, regardless of how the overall market condition is, because it is supposedly about your time in the markets, not timing the markets. Basically, the message is always geared at giving them your money, keeping it with them and never taking it away, so they can continuously charge you various fees. At the end of the day, if the client makes money, all the better, but even if they don't, the individual and company still gets to charge their fees.

In providing Genuine Investment Advice verses Poor Investment Advice, an individual's salary and bonus often comes in between the two. I'm reminded of a quote from Upton Sinclair: "It is difficult to get a man to understand something, when his salary depends on his not understanding it." However, to be fair, many of those who work in the financial and investment industry are not unscrupulous or ill-intentioned. Like many everyday people, they too, are caught up in the confusion. They come across poor investment advice that they actually believe to be true, which they use themselves and also end up passing on.

ADDITIONAL INVESTMENT TIPS FOR THE EVERYDAY INVESTOR

Make Use of Technical Analysis

As individual investors, we have limited time and resources. I believe the most efficient and effective way for an individual investor to conduct market research and to look for investment opportunities is through the use of technical analysis. Before you get intimidated, technical analysis is basically a fancy way of saying to look at price charts and graphs. You are literally looking at a picture, the big picture. It's efficient because, for example, if I wanted to, I could literally look through hundreds of companies and their price charts in a day. Comparatively, I cannot read through hundreds of annual reports or articles a day.

Keep an Investing Journal

Experiencing losses due to bad judgements or mistakes is part of every investor's journey. Unfortunately, when it comes to investing, making mistakes usually translates to losing money. At least when losses and mistakes occur, try to profit from them by keeping a journal of what happened and how, in an effort to learn from the experience and to not to let it happen again. As the saying goes, "Fool me once, shame on you. Fool me twice, shame on me."

Be Sure to Diversify

Diversification is a simple risk management technique we should all make use of to protect ourselves from the unknown and to improve our risk to return ratio. The simple reason being we can never foresee and predict everything in the markets. During my years of investing, I've seen an oil company whose oil rig was destroyed by a natural disaster; a factory that, due to some employee's negligence, was burned down to a crisp; the CEO of a company who got caught up in various alleged scandals leading to the collapse of the company and, one of my favorites, which is when Tesla's stock price took a sudden dive one day because Elon Musk decided to announce that the company was going bankrupt as an April Fool's Day joke in 2018. No matter how much in-depth research we conduct, nobody could have foreseen any of those events happening. So protect your investment portfolio by diversifying.

Look Beyond "Glam Stocks"

When individuals share their investment holdings with me, I often notice that they have many of the same stock holdings. The reason is they often have what I call "Glam Stocks." These are the glamorous stocks we often hear about in the news and media, the ones our friends and family talk about at dinner parties and gatherings. There is nothing wrong with having those holdings per se, but expand your scope, look further and dig deeper. You will realize that there are plenty of more diverse opportunities out there, many of which are either less volatile and less risky, have more growth potential, have a better performance record or sometimes all of the above. So keep looking and don't settle just for what you hear or see around you.

Know When to Get Out, Before You Get In

Before you get into an investment position, decide when you would exit if things do not go as intended. You are more clear minded before you start an investment. So decide when you would exit if things do not go your way ahead of time, as you will lose objectivity afterwards.

Gradually Ease In and Out of Investments

When investing, especially in stocks, a common practice is to use one entry and one exit into an investment position. Instead of using an all-in or all-out approach, a more strategic risk management approach would be to gradually ease yourself in and out of an investment depending on its subsequent performance. For example, instead of investing $5,000 all at once, consider investing initially only $2,500, then decide if you still want to invest the remaining $2,500 depending on the subsequent performance of the particular investment. Doing this would automatically cut your initial risk by 50%. The same idea applies to getting out of an investment.

Cut Losses and Keep Them Small

When investing, keeping control of our losses is a vital component of risk management. If there is one common piece of advice I've gathered from many great investors, it is that they all cut their losses and keep them small. Considering that most big losses usually started off as small losses, there is no point in letting a small loss grow into a big loss. If you are uncertain about an investment holding, instead of holding all of it or none of it, consider selling a portion of it. For example, if you sell half of it, you will reduce your risk by 50%. Another common culprit that leads investors to hold onto losses is focusing on break-even points and prices. In reality, nobody actually cares where or at what price you bought an investment and where you would break-even. It has no special meaning to anybody other than you and the tax department, so do not focus on that.

Avoid Adding to Losing Positions

When you have a losing investment position, often people believe that buying more will get you better value as you average down your overall price point. That is actually a poor strategy because having a losing position usually means that something you anticipated did not materialize and instead the opposite outcome occurred. There must have been something that was misjudged, overlooked, or unforeseen. Therefore, it does not make strategic sense to add more to an investment which you have already misunderstood and misjudged. Moreover, not only does that go against the concept of keeping your losses small, it is in fact the opposite, because you are adding more money to a losing position.

Remember that You Are Investing in Your Beliefs, Not the Markets

If there is one piece of advice that is more important than controlling your losses, it would definitely be that nobody cares more about your financial well-being than you. So understanding finance and investments is a life skill you should not only acquire but develop, and it all starts with your beliefs. At the core of it all, it is about working on developing your investment belief system.

This requires realigning and readjusting your beliefs and perhaps adopting new ones that serve you, while discarding those that do not. Remember that at the end of the day, we are all just investing in our beliefs.

FINAL THOUGHTS

Finance and investments are one of my greatest passions. I hope I was able to share some fresh perspectives and unique insights on subjects that I personally find to be rarely touched upon or discussed. The ideas and concepts are not exhaustive or complete, however, these are the big ideas, essential concepts and quintessential core beliefs that I've acquired through the years and which really helped propel my investment understanding and financial success.

Often there is nothing worse than to listen to someone advising you on how to reach your goals, when they have not actually reached it themselves. If there was a way for me to turn back time and have the opportunity to sit down with some successful investors who were willing to give me a few important pointers about finance and investing over a cup of coffee or a meal, I hope they would have shared with me the same pointers and beliefs I have shared with you in the last few pages. I know the insights would have definitely made my investment and financial experience a lot smoother and would have helped me reach my financial goals a lot sooner. These beliefs I'm talking about have helped me through many hurdles, make many investment breakthroughs and achieve financial success. I hope they will do the same for you. Remember, "It's Possible!"

For more investment insight, techniques and strategies, visit:

InvestingItWisely.com

Your Life Energy

AMAL INDI

I have 20 years of experience in the tech sector and corporate banking. In my previous life in the "Rat Race", I was waking up every day and going to a job that provided well for me. After some major changes in my life (including a divorce), I started recognizing that I wasn't intrinsically happy. I would be going about my day filled with negative thoughts and emotions. It felt as though they were taking over in a way, and I recognized how they were beginning to affect every moment of my day and every interaction with those around me. I refer to these as "Thought Bugs", which I will go on to explain later. These Thought Bugs were almost like a computer virus, affecting all the thoughts or, as one may say, programming in my mind. After recognizing these Bugs and studying them in myself for many years, I began to draw strong conclusions about how I could create positive change in my mind. This positive change in my thoughts would eventually lead to me leaving the "Rat Race" and starting on the mission of my life to share my new paradigm with those around me. I believe that we can change our minds and create a positive and uplifting life, not only for ourselves, but for those around us. I would love to share with you the basics of what I discovered, a new way of examining our thought patterns and how to drastically shift the energy around you (your Aura) so that you can lead a fantastic life!

GETTING STARTED ON YOUR OWN JOURNEY

When was the last time you really felt 100%? When I say 100%, I mean you wake up feeling a general positivity in your mood, you are looking forward to a new day, your interactions with people feel good, and you walk around feeling a general sense of purpose even with the simple tasks of getting groceries or whatever your work environment. You may think that you have no say in how you really feel. That deep down, you cannot control your thoughts and emotions. I know that this is not true. I developed a unique way of seeing our minds and how deeply they affect our energy. Have you heard of life energy, such as positive energy, negative energy, Aura energy, and universal energy? Read on!

WHAT MAKES US HUMAN?

Each one of us is a biological marvel of different cells, tissues, genes. These are the many working pieces that come together to create our human body. What really makes us human in a whole sense? We each possess an in-depth energetic landscape that we can't deny. This energetic pulse is used by scientists and technicians daily to perform tests and create pictures of our bodies and their functions. Think of the neuroscientists that connect our bodies to electrodes and measure our brain waves. That's part of it. We can't deny there is a part of us beyond just the tissues of our muscles and bones.

Did you know that surrounding you right now is an energy field that is all your own? This energetic field is referred to as your Aura. This Aura can be the beginning of a life that you love. Every human being has an energy field around them. We cannot see this field with the naked eye. However, we can see this field with an Aura machine. It's true! I personally have had mine captured and what was reflected back to me (in terms of energetic levels) was what I was truly feeling.

Your Aura and the energy you radiate is 100% in your control. Some days, you might feel positive and good, while other days, you may feel more negative and lower. These are your energy levels. They can vibrate high or low. It depends on you and your thoughts. Remember, with improvements to your mind and thoughts, your aura energy field will continuously change, thus altering the life you are leading.

YOUR AURA

Over the centuries of humans existing and contemplating our existence, many have acknowledged the fact that we have an energy that extends beyond our skin and flesh, which can actually interact with the world around us. This is referred to as your body's Aura. The Aura refers to the energy around your body that can be affected from the inside out or the outside in. When it is strong, the Aura around your body can extend quite a way beyond the barrier of your physical body (your skin). It can also manifest as different colours, depending on the emotional mood of the person. For example, when you are in a state of calm, then you will exude a white Aura. When you are in a state of anger, then you will exude a red Aura. Sometimes Auras may also be a combination of different colours. There is technology now that can show the colour and strength of someone's Aura. I have had mine checked. One day, it was light in colour and extended far beyond my body. This didn't surprise me as I feel I live in a state of calm, clear energy and my inner emotional landscape is positive. If you were to have an opportunity to get yours checked today what do you think the results would be? Strong and white? Or weak and maybe red? Maybe you feel like it may not show up at all.

This is what I want to teach you. This is my mission right now: To help you understand that you can empower yourself and create a strong, positive Aura that will not only affect your overall sense of well-being. It will affect your relationships, your business, and your life as a whole.

YOUR HUMAN SYSTEM

Through my own exploration, I began seeing and noticing a pattern in how my Aura was being affected by different things in my life. As I continued to study this in myself, it became clear to me that that there were specific things in play, and it was all rooted in my mind. Having a strong background in technology, I began to clearly see how our own minds behave like supercomputers. (Stay with me here!) Just like a super computer, we have our own operating system and the ability to run many programs at once. We are constantly juggling responsibilities, taking in the world around us, assessing how we feel, and determining what we need. The list could go on and on! Just take a moment right now: close your eyes and connect to all the "programs" open in your mind that are constantly running. Relate that to being connected to your own unique operating system of your mind. Now imagine that a computer virus was implanted into one of your programs and began affecting your thoughts. Computer viruses are designed to spread to all parts of a computer with the goal of eventually changing the computer, more often than not, making it completely dysfunctional. This is what can happen in your mind. A negative thought may enter your mind about something specific. Maybe a co-worker engages you in conversation about a rumour that someone is up for raise (one that you applied for) or on your coffee break the barista makes a mistake on your order and you feel it ruins your morning. I call these viruses of our thoughts Human Errors. In its most basic form, Human Errors can be outlined as the following emotions, or what I like to call Thought Bugs:

- Anger
- Suspicion
- Craving
- Comparison
- Low self-esteem
- Procrastination
- Getting stuck in negative thoughts

What it can be boiled down to is that these negative thought bugs can enter into your mind, which in turn creates negative energy. This leads to stress and a weakening of your Aura.

I'm sure you can think of a definitive moment, probably even within the last day or the last week, where you can see how your own errors were affecting your core system and negatively impacting the energy around you.

Luckily, we have a set of more positive emotions and various ways of reacting that counter the negative ones. I have identified these and aptly named them our Human Features.

Primary Human features that combat the errors include:

- Love and kindness
- Acceptance
- Forgiveness
- Courageousness
- Patience
- Authenticity
- Gratefulness

One can think of these features as a built-in tool box to combat negativity. This is always at our disposal! I want to help you identify where these positive emotions are in you, so that you may have access them and strengthen the energy that you are putting out into the world and your Aura.

Look, I am not a psychologist. I am not a therapist. I am, however, a believer in how we show up to our work and interact with those around us will have a deep impact on the life we are creating for ourselves. I have firsthand experience. I have taken myself from a place of negativity and darkness to a place of possibility. I have watched my newfound passions and work flourish, along with my relationships, personal and otherwise.

This is a different way of looking at things. This just isn't your usual "Be positive" message. This is connecting into the fact that as humans, we have a distinct design in place to help us truly create a good life for ourselves. The foundation of this is to truly feel happy and positive from the inside out, so that what we engage with is affected by our positive energy. Think of the last time you had an encounter with someone who you felt emitted a positive or happy energy? How did it make you feel? How did you react? You truly have the power to combat these negative thought processes (bugs) already in you! Don't you want to be the one truly living in your potential and sharing your positivity with everyone and everything in your life?

THE "AWESOME LIFE" IS WAITING FOR YOU!

Let's get down to business. Thanks for sticking with me. If you have continued reading to this point, then I want to applaud you! It means that you are deeply interested in living your best life.

Side effects of a mind free from negative Thought Bugs may include:

- General feelings of happiness and relaxation
- Genuine connections when meeting people
- A mind free from clutter
- A deep appreciation for the world and people around you
- High levels of productivity
- Willingness to learn new skills
- Gaining more contacts and connections with ease
- Feeling an authentic excitement for projects and self-development
- Being ready to rock your life!

These are just a few of the feelings available to you if you commit to removing negative Thought Bugs from your life, thus strengthening your energy and Aura from the inside out. I wouldn't be here today if I didn't do the work and experience the benefits of being on the other side of the process.

BRING LIGHT TO YOU

My hope for you is to learn how to identify your negative Thought Bugs and stop their process of multiplication. For you to empower yourself with positivity and strengthen your aura. For you to leave feelings of depletion behind and bring your energy back to 100%. For you to share your positive energy with the world and make it a better place!

Never forget: An Awesome Life is within your reach at all times. I believe it. In fact, I will go so far as to say I know it is. I have taken my own life and made it awesome by taking all I have outlined in my work and applying it to myself. Now it is your turn to turn up the positivity in your life and let your Aura shine!

I encourage you to check out my website, www.happinessmountain.com, to receive a free guide on removing your negative energy. In this guide, you will also be given a sneak peek into the app I am developing. The Happiness Mountain™ app will quickly become your new best friend! I developed the Happiness Mountain™ app to be a way to actually track those negative Thought Bugs and coach you to clear your worries and boost your energy levels! By giving you this important tool at your fingertips, I know you will be able to strengthen your energy and basically start living a more happy life! If you haven't guessed already, I love technology and its possibilities for enhancing our lives. I can't wait for you to be one of the first people to try this app and reap its benefits right away at www.happinessmountain.com/app.

BRINGING LIGHT TO YOU SO THAT YOU MAY BRING LIGHT TO THE WORLD

Now that I have given you some insight on how you can truly change your life by changing your own energy, I want to share the ways that Happiness Mountain™ can help you begin to apply these concepts. The process of understanding, application, and execution is key when committing to changing the way your mind functions and, over time, changing your aura.

Now that you know you have the power to change your life via your thoughts, I wonder why you wouldn't want to act now to change your life. Your own personal idea of an awesome life is within reach! I left behind an old way of living and being in order to start on a new path. I am confident that you have the power to do that for yourself as well. We all just need a little help. To be honest, I wish I had connected with these deeper levels of understanding regarding my thoughts and how they affect my life earlier. However, as we all know, timing is everything, especially when it comes to your advancement on both a personal level and a business one. Take this as a sign that it may be time for you to dive into these deep changes. The techniques, once you really begin to understand them, are quite straightforward. I know that you live a busy life and are striving to do your best. However, it takes commitment to change. Why not start now?

Happiness Mountain™ can offer you many tools to get started and help you dive deeper. The first step is easy! I encourage you to head over to my website www.happinessmountain.com to sign up and stay connected to the developments in my work. You will automatically receive an easy to follow guide on how to remove your negative energy, which will be delivered right to your inbox! You will also be given an automatic sneak peek into my app.

THE HAPPINESS MOUNTAIN™ APP

I am constantly inspired by how we connect online through different platforms and technologies. I believe that this can be the start to a great change in how we grow and develop. I designed the app as a convenient way for you to connect to your energy boosting practices on the go. We all spend some time on our phones scrolling and engaging on different platforms. Why not invest that time mindfully instead of mindlessly? The Happiness Mountain™ app, www.happinessmountain.com/app, helps you do that by having the tools you can utilize to boost your own positive energy available at any time!

Features include the following:

- Troubleshooting what is worrying you and replacing that worry with positivity
- Ways to resolve disputes without creating negative energy and affecting your Aura
- Aura boosting activities you can do on daily basis, while tracking your progress with your own private point system
- An emergency toolkit for handling sudden negative situations
- An easy guide to all the Thought Bugs and how to handle them available at a touch of your screen, so that you may continue to learn how you can change your thoughts to more positive ones and keep your positive energy high!

HAPPINESS MOUNTAIN™ FOR KIDS

Calling all parents and anyone who takes care of children! This work isn't just applicable to more mature minds and bodies. It can start when we are young! I am in the process of finishing development on a series of books for children that will cover all the core concepts of my work and Happiness Mountain™, so that we may share these valuable tools and concepts even with the developing minds of the next generation. Of course, there will be interactive games for children as well, because as we all know that some of the best learning happens when we are having fun! This goes for adults too, don't you think? Stay in the loop by connecting with me at www.happinessmountain.com.

MY NEXT BOOK

I am ready to dive deeper and share with you even more in my new book, *Happiness Mountain™: Double Your Happiness, Awesomeness and Spirituality*. In the book we are going to explore deeper than ever before. *Happiness Mountain™* will go more in depth on how you can harness the three levels of energy (Positive/Negative, Aura and Universal) to change your perspective and unlock your perfect life. I want to share with you the techniques and deep processes that will affect all aspects of your life. Remember those 'Negative Thought Bugs' I was talking about earlier? In my new book I will teach you not only how to eliminate them, I want to teach you how to protect yourself from future encounters with 'Negative Thought Bugs' therefore truly creating change in your life for the better. You will also learn techniques on how to recharge your energy, boost your aura and use your new skills for resolving conflicts and affecting your business.

I want you to harness the power of your personal Positive & Aura energies, learn to dance with the Universal energy that is always at your disposable and be able to live at a level of existence that falls in line with your ideal, perfect life. Take a look at the *Happiness Mountain™* diagram on the next page. You can define your perfect life as living with a high level of inner peace, the level of inner happiness. Your Awesome Life and Spiritual Life revolves around being of service to others and helping others. You can live a combination of all levels of the *Happiness Mountain™*. Whatever you personally define as perfection is where you have the power.

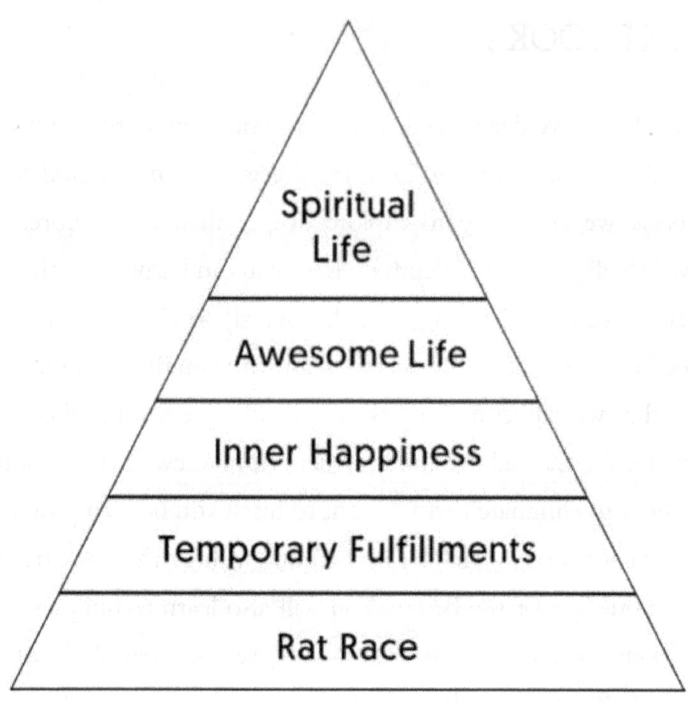

Happiness Mountain™ created by Amal Indi

Some might argue you cannot have a perfect life. I say you already have a perfect life and it is blocked by negative energy from coming into full fruition. This negative energy can be existing as a low self-esteem bug or a comparison bug. You may define perfect life as comparing to others. You may try to achieve things with craving energy. Please remember: You are already whole, complete and perfect. You cannot access your full power because of the negative energy being generated by your thoughts. When you learn to remove those negative thoughts as I teach you in *Happiness Mountain™*, you will realize how much power you have in life. This will be your turning point to harness the energy to power-up your personal, business and spiritual life! In the book I will give you all the tools and techniques to accomplish that. After reading my new book *Happiness Mountain™* you will be able to shift your life to a new paradigm that is not only accessible but exciting. How do you think it will feel to lead a perfect life? Can you think of even one thing that may change for the better if you decided to investigate how you could crush your negative energies, enhance your positive energies and essentially eliminate future worries from your life? ... Wow! I am excited for you just thinking about it myself! I know the profound changes it created for me in my life and I look forward to hearing how it affects yours.

YOU CAN LEAD AN AWESOME LIFE

My hope for you is to learn how to identify your negative Thought Bugs and stop their process of multiplication. For you to empower yourself with positivity and strengthen your aura. For you to leave feelings of depletion behind and bring your energy back to 100%. For you to share your positive energy with the world and make it a better place!

Never forget: The Awesome Life is within your reach at all times. I believe it. In fact, I will go as so far to say I know it is. I have taken my own life and made it perfect in my eyes by taking all I have outlined in my work and applying it to myself. Again, your negative thoughts may say your life is not perfect, which might include your low self-esteem, cravings, or comparison bugs blocking you. Don't let these bugs create negative energy. Instead, clear them and power-up the personal, business, or spiritual aspects of your life. Never forget you have the power over your own mind- NOT your negative Thought Bugs. Now it is time to power-up the positivity in your life and let your Aura shine!

I encourage you to check out my website, www.happinessmountain.com, for the opportunity to stay connected to the global community of people who have already begun to use this work to boost their positivity and create their

Awesome Life in their personal, business, and spiritual domains. I can't wait for you to begin using The Happiness Mountain™ App to start training your energy to stay positive and even get stronger. Of course, I encourage you to visit www.happinessmountain.com to stay connected and be in the know as to what is coming down the pipeline with this life changing work.

I have dedicated my life to bringing these concepts and work to you. I know you can change your energy and begin to not only affect your own life, but the entire world. I believe deeply that when as many people as possible align their energy to a higher, more positive state, then we can truly make a collective difference. Let's start today!

Amal Indi lives in Vancouver, Canada, and is the founder and CEO of Happiness Mountain™ Inc. After 20 years of working in technology and corporate banking, Amal is on a mission to give people the possibility to live with their full potential in their personal, business, and spiritual domains. He has found innovative techniques and tools to remove negative energy and power up your personal life, business life, and spiritual life. Ultimately, you can make the world a more awesome place for everyone. He believes that technology has the potential to transform the minds and energy of people and facilitate change. Amal wants to help people around the globe live a positive and enriching life through the energy-based tools and techniques of this innovative system he has developed to strengthen your energy and help you live a life full of happiness and potential. Find his story and work at www.happinessmountain.com.

Nobody Got Time For That!

The Ultimate Guide For Smart Money Management

URSULA GARRETT

Save, save, save! That's all you hear from family, friends and the media. You are strongly encouraged to save, but how are you supposed to save with a low-paying job, high student loan debt, and the rising cost of housing? Something has got to give – and it's usually not you giving to your savings account. Who has time to be broke when you are young and just want to have fun and enjoy your life? I'll tell you who – nobody. Nobody has got time for that, especially you!

Finances absolutely play a huge part in your life choices and opportunities. Money issues consume chunks of your brain power every day. Think of how many times money (or a lack of it) factors into your decisions throughout your fast-paced day. For instance, you schedule a date on Tinder, buy movie tickets on Fandango and make dinner reservation using Open Table, and you haven't even gotten out of bed yet to start your day. You can do this if you have money in your bank account or power (available credit) on your credit card. Yes, either method of payment will get you what you want right now – one is a smart choice and the other, not so much. You must make smart choices regularly, there is no getting around it.

Size does matter, especially when it refers to your bank account. I want you to recognize that money underwrites the type of life you live and the lack of it means you're not living the life you want to be living. You are forced to make hard choices about what you can afford or what you have to give up. Having limited options make you feel as if your life is less than it could be. Smart money management is the key to your financial goals and personal goals aligning.

Once you recognize that the choices you make with your finances are either limiting your options or providing you opportunities, you can start being more proactive with your finances. First, it is important for you to understand how easy it is to handle your personal business, so you can create real changes that will significantly impact your life.

Two of my five daughters are about the same age, 26 (not twins just a blended family). Throughout their lives, they have taken different paths and made different choices. They are in their mid-twenties now and both spend more than they should, however, one is contributing to a retirement plan and has money go directly from her paycheck into a savings account. The other one lives paycheck to paycheck, has no retirement savings, no personal savings, and is regularly subsidized by her parents. Three guesses which one has more opportunities to live the life she wants, and the first two guesses don't count. While they each had similar opportunities, their individual choices have dictated their current circumstances.

"I am not a product of my circumstances. I am a product of my decisions."

- Stephen Covey

It's a bit of a mystery why you make some of the decisions you make and that's especially true when it comes to your finances. I can tell you from experience that a crystal ball, mesmerizing though it may be, is not where you will find those answers. How often have you made poor financial choices in the moment, only to later regret them and wonder how you got into this situation again? Well, I'm here to tell you that it doesn't matter how or why, what matters is what you do to fix it and make sure it never happens again.

If you have ever paid attention to political elections, then you know how easily you can be fooled by your assumptions, fears and false intuitions. I say this to help you understand that listening to others' opinions about what you should do won't help you reach your goals. Making a plan and following through will.

Which is why I find it useful to understand some principle concepts when you make decisions about money. This is besides, of course, the regular practices of following a budget, saving, investing and avoiding most kinds of debt, factors that I will discuss as part of the steps for smart money management.

These four concepts are the foundation you need for your decision-making process when you are creating your budget or making the decisions about those investments and savings plans. They need to factor into all your financial decisions, because they will help keep you from sabotaging your financial stability.

1) OPPORTUNITY COSTS

No matter what you do or the opportunities that you pursue, there is always going to be a cost. You have to give something to get something. Nothing in life is free. Individually, we get to decide what we are willing to give in exchange. In some circumstances, the price is simply too high, or the payoff is too low to make the deal or take the chance. That threshold is different for everyone and is based on your values.

For example, deciding whether or not to pursue higher education is a decision you make based on your priorities, which could include your financials, your time, and your perception of the value of higher education. Pursuing an advanced degree may take years -- are you willing to put in that amount of time? It could involve giving up other opportunities to finish your degree, but at the same time, the network you build could allow you access to individuals who can create even greater career opportunities in the future. Many individuals choose their university based on the alumni and the type of network they can access for mentors.

Additionally, there is the debt that often comes with pursuing higher education. Are you willing to put yourself into that kind of debt, the type of debt that will take years to pay off? Many individuals see their degree as a doorway to career advancement in a specific field or as a way to pursue the type of work that they are passionate about. For them, the cost of the degree in terms of finances and time is worth it, because they see that degree as an investment in their long-term financial future.

Those two daughters I mentioned earlier, one went to college and has a degree in business and some student loan debt. The other worked part-time jobs and traveled to visit friends she met on the internet. One daughter wanted a college degree and was willing to sacrifice four years of her life, accumulate debt (she considered it as an investment) and forego immediate travel opportunities. The other daughter thought that price was too high. This isn't a matter of right or wrong but a matter of what you are willing to give to get what you want. Here is a general rule of thumb: The bigger the opportunity, the greater the cost or sacrifice to achieve it.

Every decision that you make has all those considerations and it is up to you to give them all a voice before you make your decision. At the same time, your priorities need to guide those smaller financial decisions that we all make throughout the day. Many of your long-term goals are going to be impacted by your short-term decisions. Therefore, giving yourself guidelines for daily spending based on your priorities will help you to reach those goals. Still, not everything can be quantified in terms of your return on investment, as I will explore next.

2) SUNK COSTS

What is sunk cost? This is money you can't get back -- a non-refundable airline ticket, for example. There are certain expenses that you will have throughout your life that are not going to bring a tangible return on investment. In fact, they are likely going to result in nothing more than an enjoyable experience or a pleasant memory. It can be easy to get into a mindset that has you spending far beyond what you may have budgeted or prioritized because you value the experience, but it can put you in a financial bind later. The idea here is that you need to keep sunk costs in proper perspective. It's easy to start thinking, "Well, I've already spent $100, so what's another $25?" My mother always told me not to throw good money after bad. She taught me to understand the concept of sunk costs long before I took a business class. You have got to be willing to walk away sometimes and keep the money in your pocket for other investment opportunities.

Once something is paid for, and cannot be refunded, it shouldn't impact your future financial decisions. It is a "sunk" cost, i.e. water under the bridge, and no matter what you do in the future you won't ever get it back. Therefore, you can't allow yourself to get hung up on the moments where you spent money in a way that didn't fall into your overall financial plan. In the end, you have to accept that sunk costs are going to happen and make your peace with them. Recognize that you will buy emotionally and defend rationally, even if that might not always be wise. There are costs that are simply not recoupable.

Regrets over sunk costs can make it harder to move forward, leaving you vulnerable to make other choices that you may not have otherwise made. Do not allow yourself to fall into the downward spiral. Negative thoughts often breed more negative thoughts, especially if you continue to dwell on them. The same can be said for financial decisions. When you focus on your bad financial decisions, you may find yourself repeating them, because that is your focus.

It is important to keep yourself focused on ways to improve your financial decisions and keep them in line with your financial plan. Yes, you might regret a decision, but make the conscious choice not to dwell on it. Instead, learn from it and move forward. Life, especially when it comes to finances, is a series of learning experiences. The better you are at accepting the lessons, the better decisions you will be able to make in the future. I find inspiration and humor in the lyrics of one of my favorite songs by Chumbawamba, "I get knocked down, but I get up again, you're never gonna keep me down."

Now that you have that mindset (and that song stuck in your head), you can keep yourself from making financial decisions based on your sunk costs and focus on maximizing your earnings. That starts by focusing on finding the right investments for you. With that in mind, let's talk about the Rule of 72.

3) QUICK INTEREST CALCULATIONS USING THE RULE OF 72

One of your biggest concerns about an investment should be, "What am I going to get out of this?" While you wouldn't want to ask that of a date, it's perfectly acceptable, in fact it's expected, to ask that of a potential investment. All of us want a way to determine the upside of a financial opportunity. Now there are several ways to analyze a financial investment, but it often comes down to how long it will take for an investment to pay off. Want to double your holdings? The Rule of 72 can tell you how long it will take, based on the specific interest rate. Just divide 72 by the interest rate to learn how long it will take to double your initial investment.

For example, if you are looking at an investment with an interest rate of 6 percent, then 72 divided by 6 gets you 12 years. You can then take that information and use it to determine if that timeframe will work with your overall financial plan. Granted, you may find that other factors will play a part in determining your return as well, but it is important to have an idea of what you can expect before you put money into an investment.

This is a rough estimate, of course, but it's pretty effective. Recognize that you might find that a return is going to take significantly longer to make you money. So even if you find it an interesting opportunity, you may opt to not invest in order to take advantage of a different opportunity that will give you a faster return on your money.

In fact, you can also turn the equation around to determine the interest rate you are looking at if someone promises to double your returns in a set amount of time. Twice as much money in 12 years? Divide 72 by 12 and you get an interest rate of 6 percent. This rule lets you evaluate investment opportunities quickly and decide where to put your money in a way that will help you to grow your investments to meet long-term financial goals.

Keep in mind, future earnings are not something that you can count on, so how you use the dollars that you have now are going to have greater weight than potential earnings. You know that old saying, "Don't count your chickens before the eggs hatch."

4) THE TIME VALUE OF MONEY

According to this concept, a dollar you receive today is worth more than a dollar you will get tomorrow. You will have opportunity to invest that dollar immediately and begin earning more revenue from it (and also avoid losing value because of inflation).

It is important to recognize that money from your investments needs to be put to work. Don't be quick to spend it. Making frivolous or useless purchases means you are making a choice to spend on meaningless things and activities and in doing so, you are draining your ability to invest and grow. Focus on how you can essentially create a chain of investments, all working to grow an income stream for you to use in retirement or even for a big purchase that is part of your financial plan (think a house or car). Growth is a long-term process and it is imperative that you do make the time for it.

When you are waiting for an investment to pay off, then you are waiting for your money to work for you. One of the ways that you can save money is by limiting your interest payments. When you are making money from investments, which is then reinvested, you create an income stream that can allow you to pay cash for items, or put down a larger down payment, thus helping to reduce those interest payments, or eliminate them altogether.

Again, this helps you make certain calls about your purchases -- and your income. It's the old "one bird in the hand is worth two in a bush" theory in action for your wallet.

These four concepts have served me well over the years. Now let's focus in on the five steps that will help you to remain financially sound as you invest and grow your income to meet your financial goals.

WHY MONEY MATTERS

Before I talk about the steps, I want you to understand that money has a place and purpose in your life. Whatever adventures or experiences you want to have, you are going to need money to do it. That money is also going to be a key part of fulfilling your life's purpose, simply because money is a resource that can help you get things done. Regardless of if your goal in life is to have a non-profit that helps others or to create a company to bring a product or process to market, the truth is that money will be a resource that you need.

Since you and I can agree on that, let's start talking about your financial goals by first talking about your life goals.

STEP 1 - BUDGETING: YOUR PERSONAL BUSINESS PLAN

You have goals you want to accomplish, experience, and create in this life. This is simply a reality we all share. By defining your goals, you are able to determine what financial moves are necessary to achieve them. Too often, personal goals are overlooked or under-appreciated when creating a financial plan. Your personal goals and your financial plan need to be in sync for you to be successful at achieving either one.

For instance, if you know that your financial plan is going to allow you to achieve your personal goals, then it will help you maintain the excitement and vision you have for your life. This knowledge will help keep up the momentum during tough times or difficult circumstances when you are making sacrifices.

Budgeting should be the first part of your financial plan, because it will show the money you have coming in and going out. Once you understand your cash flow, then you have all the information you need to make a sound financial plan. Your budget will allow you to make good choices about how you want to use your money and where you can make changes in your spending habits to align your personal goals with your financial goals.

As part of that budgeting process, you need to look at the choices you make on a daily basis. Consider that if you take out that Tinder date on Saturday night maybe you can't afford to play golf on Sunday. If you really want to golf, then maybe you have to Netflix and chill with $1 bottles of beer or a $7 bottle of wine and takeout pizza instead of your dinner and a movie date. We all have to make choices. Just make sure your choices are good choices. You may find that you are sabotaging yourself by the financial decisions you make every day.

The good news is that you don't have to try to figure out a budget on your own or hire a professional to do it for you. All you need is that device that sometimes acts as another appendage – your cell phone. Yes, there is another reason that your cell phone is your best friend because there's an app for that (for budgeting, that is). Actually, there are several apps for that, you just have to choose the one that works best for you.

I use Mint to track my personal bank accounts, credit cards, investments and bills – it creates a budget based on my income and expenses and reminds me when I have a payment due date. I love that my whole financial life is accessible in one place and that I can monitor activity at a glance. One of my daughters uses Clarity Money, which has similar features plus the added benefit of helping to cancel unwanted subscriptions. With an app, you won't have to wonder if you are spending too much money shopping or eating out, you can see it in full color. Knowledge is power, and this knowledge can be used to change your spending behavior to match your financial goals.

For instance, think about that $5 cup of coffee you stop to buy every morning to start your day. That money falls into the sunk costs pot, because you are not getting that money back and it is not working for you. Imagine how much money you could save if you took that $5 per day for a year and saved or invested it – you would have more than $1,825. Going back to those two daughters of mine, one likes to buy and play internet games, a lot – can you guess which one? I'll tell you it's not the one that uses Clarity Money. If you are having trouble saving to meet your long-term goals, then it might be worth exploring using an app to help you get control of your spending.

It is not about giving up your lifestyle, but making your lifestyle adhere to your financial priorities, instead of letting your lifestyle dictate your priorities. Everyone has time to know their money.

Part of achieving any financial goal is to create a nest egg of funds to work with, which serves as a basis for your investment portfolio. Using your budget, you can designate a specific percentage to go into your savings.

STEP 2 – SAVING

The point of saving is to create a financial resource that you can use to build your income streams. These income streams can be diversified, but the point is that saving has to be a priority in order to improve your financial situation and allow you to reach your goals. Here are just a few reasons why saving is important.

1. You have a nest egg for emergencies. Time and time again, financial emergencies have sunk individuals who appear to be doing well, simply because they had nothing to fall back on. Once it happens, they have a financial issue, one that can have a ripple effect across other areas of their lives. Point blank, having an emergency, such as an unexpected car repair or house repair, should not financially sink you. Experts recommend that your savings for emergency needs to cover six months of your living expenses. Once you reach that goal, keep saving a set amount to grow your emergency fund. If you have to use some of it for an emergency, then replace it as soon as possible.

2. You can save for larger purchases. You know that paying cash for items can save you money in the long run, because you won't pay interest on top of the purchase cost. When you designate savings for specific

purchases, it allows you to reach your financial goals without acquiring payments. Plus, once you make that big purchase, you can start saving for the next big item or event.

3. You can save to invest to build income streams. Once you have achieved your emergency savings goal, start building a savings that is specifically for investments. These funds should not be used for any other purpose, allowing you to adjust the rate of return to meet your goals.

Clearly, saving is important because it gives you a stepping stone to meet your financial needs and personal dreams. Now, I want to transition to the exploring the possibilities that you can create with a savings that was started for investing.

STEP 3 – INVESTING

When you reach the point that you have started an investment savings account, you have plenty of opportunities. From stocks and bonds to direct investing in a business, you have multiple ways to grow your investment dollars. That being said, it is important to choose investments that fall in line with your goals and your risk tolerance level.

For instance, if you are at the beginning of your career, you might find yourself more inclined to look for high return, risky investments. Why? Many of those who are younger see time on their side and recognize that they have time to recover from a loss. Alternately, as you reach specific benchmarks or get closer to achieving your financial goals, you will start to make less risky investments.

Another potential scenario is that you are planning to get married or start a family, in which case, you might be more concerned with the risk of losing the primary financial provider. In a case like this, you may be more interested in investing in a disability or life insurance policy or even starting a college fund. After all, not all investments are created equal.

Where you are in your life can play a large part in what type of investments you choose to take on. Additionally, you might take on investments that are less time-consuming because they give you the ability to do more of what you enjoy. On the other hand, you might want to be more hands-on in your investments, so that may be a factor in the types of investments you choose.

Your investment plan should be personalized to you and designed to meet your needs. I want you to recognize that working with a financial advisor can help you to determine the best investments for you.

Many of the individuals I work with even consider investing in themselves, which means starting their own business. If you want to explore your entrepreneurial spirit, that can be a great way to invest and see your returns grow, using your investment dollars and sweat equity. Again, I encourage you to put any investment up against your financial plan. Ask yourself the hard questions about whether it will work towards accomplishing your goals. Doing so is critical to keeping you focused and on the path to achieving both your financial and personal goals. Just keep in mind that it takes time to grow and any time frames set by you can be changed, especially if the situation changes.

STEP 4 – AVOIDING MOST KINDS OF DEBT

Debt can drown you financially and make it difficult for you to achieve your financial goals. When you look at your budget, do you see areas where you are spending money on payments regularly? That is money which is not being used to create income streams or to reach your financial goals.

Be picky when you are choosing to take on debt. I recommend that you only finance things that will bring in money or pay for themselves. It's okay to finance your education because you expect your education to yield you a higher paying career. Do not finance your vacation because you will have nothing but memories to show for it. You can pay for your business advertising with a credit card but not your groceries. Avoid running up your credit cards, leaving yourself strapped with payments. The interest payments can quickly exceed your budget and be a drain. Use the cash in your bank account to pay for your living expenses because the interest on credit cards is usually greater than the interest you earn on money deposited in the bank.

Some debt can be beneficial and preferable because it shares the risk. I am talking about debt that involves investing. For instance, if you are building a real estate portfolio of rentals and you have $100,000 to invest, you might find that you choose to split that $100,000 into down payments for five properties instead of just buying one for $100,000. The reason is that you can increase your cash flow across five properties and they can also cover their own overhead. In the meantime, you are creating equity that you can tap into later to purchase more properties. The point is that you want to use your investment cash to maximize your income opportunities. Do not limit yourself because you want to avoid all debt – some debt can be good.

When weighing your debt options, be sure to look at interest rates. Do not feel as if you are limited to one lender or one financing option. Shop around and make sure that you get the lowest possible rate for your debt with the best payment plan to meet your investment needs. Also, make sure that any investment purchased with debt is going to have a positive cash flow. Some investments may not have a positive cash flow initially but will overtime as the debt is paid down. For other investments, it is the value which grows over time that offsets the lack of a positive cash flow.

Again, it is important to work with a professional who can help you determine what types of debt you want to take on regarding your investments and what debt you want to avoid.

In the end, this step is mostly focused on helping you to avoid debt that drains you financially, without giving you any type of return. Think about the cost of those daily coffees. The focus of this step needs to be on defining the lifestyle you want and then investing in order to be able to afford it. If you opt to live a lifestyle that drains your investments, you could be shortchanging yourself for the future, thus limiting your ability to reach your dreams.

STEP 5 – EVALUATE AND ASSESS: ONGOING PROCESS

I call this step, "the shit happens" part of your plan. Yes, it would be nice if life happened exactly as we planned it, but real life is no fairy tale. The reality is that you made a plan based on the life you wanted to live and all the messy stuff that got in your way is why you had contingency plans, emergency funds and cushions built into your plan. Shit happens, and you deal. You deal by adapting to your new situation. Update your plan as if it is a living, breathing organism.

For instance, you had an accident that kept you from working for six months. That would be both physically and financially draining. This is only a temporary setback. Now you need to reset your goals to achieve your plans, because you may need to focus on rebuilding instead of growth. Still, the point is to make adjustments that help you achieve your goals, thus not allowing the circumstances to overwhelm you and derail your finances permanently.

This need to make adjustments also applies to your investments. I recommend at least once per quarter that you review your investments to make sure they are performing as expected. You don't want to waste your resources on underperforming investments.

Are there areas you might want to expand even further, or do you need to eliminate some investments because they no longer fit your financial goals? Doing these reviews regularly can help you to keep your financial life on track with your personal life. When the two are in sync, then you will find that your life continues to improve. This harmony makes it possible to achieve what you want, no matter the setbacks you might occasionally encounter.

Keep in mind that evaluating and assessing will always be ongoing processes. The fluidity of life is that you can create plans, but events may alter those plans or even offer you new opportunities and experiences that you might not have even considered.

It is important to keep your mind open, both to new investments and to new experiences and opportunities in your personal life. They often can dovetail together more than you ever realize.

Financially, your world is built on the decisions that you make throughout your life. Always know the direction you want to go before you start your journey. When you make decisions without direction, your life will be like a boat without a rudder. It goes all over but doesn't actually get anywhere. The waves take the boat in multiple directions without a clear destination.

I want you to define your path and then work in harmony with that by making choices to complement it. Even with a defined path, it can be easy to make decisions that run contrary to your goals, as I discussed earlier in this chapter. When I work with individuals, I help them to not only define their path, but also to determine the types of goals that align with their paths. Then, I can help them to find the right investments and set financial goals to help them go further on that path.

Growth happens by learning from those people who inspire you to do and be more. We all have time to learn and grow.

Please email Ursula Garrett at ugarrett@cpagarrett.com or visit her website www.cpagarrett.com

Branding Into Greatness

ANDRE DAWKINS

We all have greatness within us. The deciding factor is our will. Nothing that happens in life has any meaning unless we CHOOSE to make it so. Are you used to making quick decisions, or do you tend to procrastinate? Do you have strong will power? Do you act on emotion or on the thoughts you consciously choose? The answers to questions like these matter a great deal when it comes to greatness. Do you choose meanings consciously? Do you choose meanings that work for you instead of against you? Or do you react to situations based on emotion? Whatever you do, remember that you always achieve when you choose to put all your might into doing something good.

I'm a mortgage broker. A great one. It's why, if you're looking into investing in real estate, you should **CALL ANDRE at 1.647.991.7325**. Consider the following …

- Instead of going to a bank for a home loan you can have me work on your behalf to both shop your rate with multiple lenders and manage your loan application from start to finish.
- Often times, when going to a bank directly to apply for a loan, you could instantly jeopardize your chance of approval by simply saying the wrong thing
- I can shop your rate for you at various banks. For example: Bank A may have the lowest mortgage rate available, Bank B may have the lowest closing costs available and Bank C may have the best combination of rate and fees.
- I'm your loan guide and can be very accessible and hands-on from start to finish, and I may find a home for your loan among my many lending partners, which is especially useful if you've been denied elsewhere. I can also provide more advanced/tailored recommendations or structure your loan favorably to lower costs.
- When it comes to your credit, I specialize in credit building and repairing, so I can provide you with a blueprint to get your credit on par.
- I can offer all types of home loans, from conventional options to non-conforming stuff. I typically offer a wide product choice because of my many partners.
- NOTE: like all other loan originators, I charge fees for my services. Additionally, I may get compensated from the lender I connect you with. But remember that I can offer competitive rates that meet or beat those of retail banks, so I should be considered alongside banks

when searching for financing. Typically, if you qualify at the bank and I arrange your mortgage, there will be no fees. I also have the ability to shop numerous lenders at once so I can find the best pricing based on your needs.

If the Bank says No ... **CALL ANDRE at 1.647.991.7325**

So the bank turns you down. This may seem like the end of the world, but it's not. There are many lenders out there, and I know a lot of them. Chances are with me to walk you through every step of the mortgage process, you'll find a home for your loan with one of my many partners. Here are some things you should know:

- All banks are not created equal. For example, every lender uses different policies and criteria when assessing your application—even if they're from the same parent company. I have access to this information and can match you up with a lender whose policies best suit your circumstances. To do this yourself, you'd have to go to each lender individually and assess their loan criteria and policies. Using me allows you to avoid this hassle and target the bank best suited to you.
- When you apply for a loan, it's crucial to realize that it will be registered on your credit file. This means you really don't want to shop around. You see, enquiries happen each time you apply for any kind of finance or credit (even entering a mobile phone contract) and can affect your ability to obtain credit in the future. Applying for loan after loan will actively destroy the likelihood that you'll ever be approved--due to the number of enquiries building up on your credit file!
- Lenders don't like serial applicants, so rather than tackling a new loan application on your own, let me match you up with a suitable product

first time around, to avoid this trap.

- Getting your ducks in a row. I'll be able to tell you what you can do to improve your chances of being approved for a loan—for example, waiting until you've been at your job a few more months before you apply, or closing the credit card with the large limit that's reducing your borrowing power.
- I'm also an expert in low-doc loans, perfect for those who are self-employed or have a hazy credit history. I'll even tell you exactly what paperwork is required, and how to get around any obstacles in the criteria set by different lenders.
- It's to my advantage to get you the best possible deal, as I want to maintain positive relationships with my lenders, thereby knowing I will never put you into a product you can't afford. My intention is to have nothing but happy clients that have only great things to say about the service they received from my team and myself, so they can refer their friends and family to have the same experience.

I'll also be hoping you give me a good review, as I build my business partly from referrals—so it's always in my best interest to do the best thing by you.

By working with me, you could secure yourself a loan with a much lower interest rate or bonus features, potentially saving you tens of thousands of dollars over the life of the loan. Whether you're an investor or a homebuyer, if you would like further information and guidance about securing finance after your bank has said no, **CALL ANDRE at 1.647.991.7325**.

WHY YOU NEED A MORTGAGE BROKER

- They're mortgage experts who provide different lenders, loan types and rates for buyers without upfront charges.

- They can offer loan and rate options that a traditional bank may not be able to.
- They gather and manage critical paperwork while coordinating loan information with relevant parties.
- They help create your loan and close your home buying transaction properly.
- They typically close on your home faster than a traditional bank.
- You're not locked into working with a mortgage broker, and if for any reason they're not providing exceptional service, you can change brokers.

MARKET AWARENESS ... IN TERMS OF HOW BRANDING HAS ALLOWED ME TO STAND OUT IN THE MARKETPLACE.

When I first started doing mortgages, it was a constant struggle. It felt like everywhere I would turn there was doubt and closed doors. It felt as if I would never see success in this industry at all.

I keep telling myself, there has got to be a way, I gave my all to carve a niche into the marketplace. It all spiralled from the moment I adopted the principle slogan "if the bank says NO WAY? Better Call Andre!" It felt as if immediately a lightbulb went off in the consumers' eyes. Now, I'm not saying that all of a sudden everyone came running to me, however, the point is with the brand evolution it created an arena for me to play in. Once I came to the realization that I had something positive here, I immediately began my quest to build brand awareness through marketing.

I first started doing door to door hand outs of flyers that I would bring to a selected area. I was on a shoestring budget and had to make it because my "Y or why" was bigger than my how. I didn't know how it was going to happen, but I knew why it needed to happen. I was fed up with mediocrity, so I began visualizing myself as being successful. I began envision the life I wanted to create through the funnelling of my mortgage business. Then I applied my foot on the gas and keep it moving. Fast forward, I am constantly working on building and evolving my brand awareness. I was once told, closed mouths don't get fed. That hit home, as I came to realize the more the market knows of your existence, then the more the market can come to you for support and service.

I stand on the principles that I am here to serve, care for and change the lives of all my clients and customers—one deal at a time.

The moment I started making sales, I reinvested into marketing. I was fortunate to be working a full time job and earning a handsome salary. Therefore, all the mortgage money I made went right into advertising. I first put an ad in a local newspaper called SHARE newspaper, then later I put an ad on a local radio station G98.7 FM. To date, I still advertise in those two mediums because it was that foundation which allowed me to have such great market penetration.

The best part is I am only warming up. I plan to become a household name where "Call Andre" becomes a brand that is well recognized by the public.

Be on the lookout for the CA Mortgage Group: we will be expanding the brand into a more user-friendly platform from a standpoint of other agents using the Call Andre systems and techniques to serve, care for and change the lives of their customers. This is so they don't have to say I'm a mortgage agent/broker at the Call Andre Mortgage Group. The sound of CA Mortgage Group will be more appealing. But don't get confused: Call Andre is here to stay. The brand, the focus, the mission, the greatness … We are here to serve.

THINGS THE BANK WON'T TELL YOU

- You don't need a high credit score to qualify for a loan. If you're under the impression that you need a 720 credit score or higher to score the home of your dreams, think again. Many mortgage lenders require a minimum score of 680 to secure a loan. If you are applying for a High Ratio (insured mortgage with less than 20% down) mortgage loan, you may even qualify with a score of 600.
- Banks claim to have the best interest rates and have your best interest at heart, so how come it is that if you go to your bank to get a mortgage, they quote you a rate? They don't give you the best rate from the beginning. Why is it that you have to then re-approach them with a competitor rate to get them to match it.
- They usually have hidden clauses in their products that they do not inform you of. For example, a collateral charge … where they register a higher amount on the title than the actual mortgage you are getting. In other words, they hold your equity hostage.
- The penalties to break your mortgage with a big bank are a lot higher than some of the same "A" lending institutions that mortgage brokers can get you into, and they are federally regulated just like a bank. They are called monoline lenders; monoline because they only have one line of business and that, of course, is mortgages. So they will not try to cross sell you and ultimately try to sink you in more debt.
- Fees and rates vary between lenders. Don't be afraid to shop around a little bit before deciding on a mortgage lender. Typically, each lender charges different origination fees and closing costs. While it may only be 5% of the purchase price of your home, that's a big chunk of change. Search for the best deal to save yourself as much money as

possible.

- Closing at the end of the month is always better. If you choose to set your closing date at the beginning of the month, you'll end up paying more "prepaid interest," which is due at closing. Set your closing date as close to the end of the month as you can to avoid paying extra upon settling.
- Longer term mortgages cost more. If you talk to any mortgage lender, they'll try to push you towards a 30-year loan. You may think that this is because it's more affordable for you. While it will cost you less on a month-to-month basis, you'll end up paying quite a bit more in interest. If you can swing the extra money, shoot for a 15- or 20-year mortgage instead.
- There are ways to take a break from your mortgage payments. When times get tough and you are struggling to make your mortgage payment, you do have options beyond foreclosure and short sales. Most lenders offer skip-a-payment or forbearance options for those who qualify. Depending on the severity of your situation, you may even be eligible to have your payments suspended for a few months.
- Don't fall for gimmicks. Even if a lender advertises a no-cost closing, there's usually a catch. Depending on the circumstances, the lender may roll the closing costs into the loan. This means that you're actually paying more for the closing costs over the life of the loan due to interest. If it's not rolled into your loan, they may charge a higher interest rate—which would also cost you more over time.
- Most of the front line staff that you and the clients are dealing with are not home owners themselves and cannot provide you with a great scope of knowledge and information because they can't speak to you from experience. They are only trained to sell you the products the bank has to offer.

CREDIT

I Specialize in credit building and repairing. Credit to me is the most important aspect of a mortgage transaction. There are three vital parts when it comes to residential lending… the property, the credit and the income. You must have two out of three working for you to get an approval.

Credit is something that needs to be branded into every student's head before they leave elementary school. In my opinion it should be taught in grade eight. The reason being is not all students end up finishing high school. However, most kids tend to complete elementary. I think that if the average Canadian was taught how important credit is throughout their whole adult life, we would have a lot less people in a position with bad credit.

It hurts my inner being when I see someone with bruised credit, especially when they are for little issues (i.e. unpaid bills, late payments, etc.).

The biggest negative effect on one's credit is usually phone bills, as most people don't realize that yes, they are reported to your credit bureau.

If you are in a rough position, of being one of the unfortunate, misguided individuals who has been plagued by the credit system. give me a call and let's discuss your situation. There are still options available to you. Believe it or not, like insurance, everyone is entitled to a mortgage. However, just like auto insurance, you pay higher premiums when your records are bad. With mortgages you pay higher rates and higher fees when your credit is bad.

I often times advertise "No job, no credit, your approved!" This is another one of my many brand slogans, however, oftentimes, people think this applies to institutional mortgages. That is clearly not the case: the only time this is applicable is with a private mortgage.

When people approach me for a mortgage, the first thing I tell them to do is pull their credit report themselves then gather the required docs, so that we can review and work out a game plan… its beyond me to know the rate of people that stop the process, simply because they feel like I am making them do too much work. My mentor once told me, anything worth having is worth working hard for… so I empower you to follow my instructions, so we can build your financial future and make your dreams of homeownership a reality.

TEAM WORK

No man is an island… I plan on adopting this principle. I am so used to being a workaholic technician that it shows up in my brand "Call Andre." Hence the reason for the brand evolution into "CA Mortgage Group." We will re-engage that marketplace and bring awareness to the community, letting them know that Call Andre is now team, a force that is to be reckoned with, as we will stand together to serve and care for our clients, changing their lives one deal at a time.

I believe team work is important in all aspects of life, especially in the real estate market place. If you think about it, when you purchase a home, you have many people on your side working with you to get you from point A – Z. Your team consists of your mortgage broker, your realtor, your lawyer, your home inspector, your home appraiser and your financial planner

It's always good to make sure you have the best players on your side working on your best interest at all times. They should have one common goal: to serve and care for your needs and to make your experience an exceptional one. That is what we strive for here at **Call Andre at 1.647.991.7325.**

Writing Your Business' Future

TONY ROMA

There are many reasons to write a book, or even a chapter in book, such as the one I've written for you here. For some people, the reason is to provide recreation for an avid reader. For other authors, writing is a means to provide self-help for people seeking an improvement or at least a change in their lives. Finally, some writers will use books as a means to assist people technically; works that serve as a sort of how-to guide. In this chapter you will find a little bit of each of those. If I do my job well in this endeavor, you will find yourself engaged but growing and learning simultaneously.

You may wonder what makes anyone qualified to direct and lead the branding of a business through the sale of a book. Fair enough. I wouldn't want to take advice of any kind without knowing what qualifications and experience the person brings to the table, especially when we're talking about the success of my business. When considering Raymond Aaron's skills in that arena, know first that that several of the works he's published have hit the best sellers list. Most recently, Double Your Income Doing What You Love topped the charts. Aaron is also one of the most highly sought professional speakers in not just the United States, but world-wide. Further qualifications include:

- NY Times Top Ten Bestselling Author of Chicken Soup For The Parents Soul
- One of only 40 teachers in the world filmed for the hit movie sensation The Secret
- Board Member of Jack Canfield's Transformational Leadership Council
- Founder of MonthlyMentor.com, independently rated as the world's most powerful mentoring service, now in its 13th year
- Founder of the interview service WealthCreatorSource.com, now in its 10th year
- Professional speaker for 27 years, having taught in USA, Canada, Mexico, NZ, Australia, England, Ireland and Dubai

And as for sales? Consider that Aaron has ranked in the top ten Affiliates during the recent Bob Proctor and Lanny Morton launch. And finally, Aaron has a record of selling $1 million of his product in 90 minutes. Clearly, this is a man who knows how to brand and market. It would be difficult for anyone to refute his ability or the wisdom of his advice.

Even outside the publishing world you can find business leaders who recommend authorship as an excellent form of branding. Market-wide, you'll discover that writing a book is a suggested practice to grow your business better. Take a look at the following statements from two businessmen who are known as leaders and experts to model.

> *"Since my book was published I've never had a shortage of clients. I have had more clients than I could realistically serve coming to my door ever since the book came out, and the ease of converting prospects into clients has risen dramatically. It's rare for somebody to contact me now when they haven't already pretty much decided that they want to work with me if they can afford me."*
>
> - C.J. Hayden, Get Clients Now!

> *"[Publishing a book] gives you the inside track to revenues you get from the status of being an author and having that credibility. The recognition is huge."*
>
> - Alan Weiss, Million Dollar Consulting

Now let's move on now to the crux of what I want to share with you, beginning with your purpose for writing a book. Are you writing for someone's recreation, to offer help, or to provide a how-to? As stated before, each of these is a valued reason to do so. Considering that you've chosen to read The Authorities, chances are you're seeking business advice and inspiration. A goal that the reader will enjoy your piece is, of course, equally important.

BENEFITS FOR YOUR BUSINESS

Let's assume we already know your book will increase your reader's business achievements. That's its purpose. This leaves us with the question of how writing can help your business, too. First, consider that authoring a book that pertains to your field of expertise will increase the level of respect from prospective clients. This is often an immediate result of just having written the book. The fresh respect can occur before the book is even read! All it takes is for readers to discover that you're not only an expert professionally as you claim but a respected author as well. That alone can launch you into a new status. Everyone wants to hire the best of the best and as a published author, you've proven that you know more than your peers.

Writing a book elevates you to a new level of awareness with your potential client base, too. Most people rely on word of mouth and advertising. These are acceptable and even effective means of getting your name out there. However, they are also commonplace. Just think about it. How often do you ignore billboards, Internet pop-ups, email spam, and junk mail? Just gloss right over them? Even television advertisements hold less sway in this age of devices that record TV programs. Traditional advertising is often just background noise, easily and often dismissed. That means it's time to stand out from your peers. Be impressive and innovative, not just informative or clever. Writing a book is an excellent means to accomplish that goal.

Establishing credibility is another strong benefit that writing a book will bring to your business. Being able to tout that you are a published author will take you far. Here's the truth: it could be that no other person in your profession can come close to your level of knowledge or proficiency, and perhaps nobody else has your drive or your commitment to customer service. These are exceptional traits you should boast and advertise. However, if your only way to compete against others is to share your reputation the same way they do, these strengths may be moot points. In fact, they may have little bearing on growing your client list altogether. Writing a book, though? That's a different game altogether. Suddenly, you have an edge over your competitors. How many of them can say they've been published? Most likely, very few have and when people learn that you successfully have done so, suddenly your credibility surpasses that of the competition.

There is another positive impression that writing a book will provide for your clients. This is one that is extremely important but too often not seen or acknowledged: organization and management. Whether they're potential, newly engaged, or long-time clients, all are seeking someone who demonstrates not only an ability to get the job done well, but also someone who does it timely and in an organized, well-managed fashion. Deadlines must be met, regardless of circumstances, and issues slipping through the cracks are unacceptable. Now, consider yourself from the clients' points of view. They already know that you provide a superior service on a regular basis, but now you've added being a published author to your list of accomplishments. That writing is a difficult and time-consuming endeavor is the widely accepted assumption, but yet you managed to do it without breaking stride in your Business' success. It may sound basic, but people recognize and appreciate that kind of effort. Every time you can put yourself out there as more capable than someone else, the more often people will come to see you as the one who deserves your business. Today, just being a little bit better than others in business makes you a lot better in the sea of sameness!

Authoring a book also gives you an opportunity to establish and share your business agenda. As you know, having an agenda is necessary for a business to become successful. However, rarely do we share our plans with our clients at large. Why is that? After all, it's an excellent way to demonstrate your self-confidence. You're saying to the world that you already know why your plans are excellent and are giving them the recipe to your success. That kind of self-assurance is rare. Be warned, however. Sharing your business agenda also requires you to be sure it is a sound one. Readers will seek what's logical, manageable, and most importantly, something they can incorporate into their own businesses to some degree. This doesn't mean that after writing the agenda you have to throw away the lock and key. That plans shift and change is expected. In fact, provided that you demonstrate the good that's come of a change, pointing it out is an excellent point you can make in your book that will impress the readers all the more.

Sharing your business agenda is not just about confidence, however. It's an opportunity to provide concrete proof of your success. You can use actual examples that illustrate your commitment to achieving your goals, regardless of how big or small they are. We're not talking about bragging here. These are facts. You set an agenda to meet certain goals…and then you met them. What better message of commitment and determination than that to send to clients? What better way to prove yourself? But don't stop at sharing with clients. Give the agenda to your employees, too. Just as clients should know your principles and goals, so should your employees. Not only does it give them an expectation of what's in store, it also makes them more emotionally invested in the company, and thereby harder workers.

Finally, know that publishing your business agenda also works to establish your brand. A well-written, organized plan identifies with precision and detail what the core models and principles of your business are. Even better, by including them in a book, you have the advantage of perfecting their presentation. You have don't have to speak off the cuff, as is sometimes the case with clients. You'll define your business even more and have a chance to sell yourself in the best possible light.

BENEFITS WITHIN THE INDUSTRY

We've covered at length how writing a book can benefit your business. It's important to acknowledge that there is value in impressing your colleagues, too. Writing can be a wellspring of many opportunities you've never considered, many of which are well paying and all of which increase your visibility.

Often authors who write about their profession are the ones chosen to speak at business conferences. They're the experts, right? Note here that in referring to speaking engagements I didn't specify what kind of business, and that was deliberate. Once your book has increased your profile, you won't be limited to your specific field. People will want to hear about your personal journey, and how you took your business from small to great. Whether you're in welding or real estate or the manufacturing of sporting goods, if you've done well the world will be anxious to know your story.

Don't stop at speaking engagements, however. As you grow in popularity and name you'll begin to accumulate material that can be used for a second or third or even fourth book. Your knowledge may also be sought on social media initiatives. This has the potential to generate a great deal of residual income. All you have to do is establish your chosen media, and then your blogs and websites can do the work for you. Don't forget instructional DVDs, teaching gigs, and paid podcasts, either. In other words, writing that one book has the potential to give you a new life altogether.

ADVICE FROM SOCRATES

"I am where you are not." This is one of Socrates' most well known quotes and its message is particularly applicable here. Often, people with a great story to tell never do so for fear that they don't have the needed skills to be successful. However, that doesn't have to be the case. Find someone who is, as Socrates would tell us, where you are not. Hire an expert to write it for you. This possibility is one people shy away from, but they shouldn't. Does it bother you to hire a plumber? An electrician? Of course not, because they are trained to do what you can't. Hiring a consultant to pen your story is no different.

There's more advantage to employing someone to write your book than you'd first think. Hiring a writer will save you an immeasurable amount of time. Again comparing the process to hiring an electrician as compared to doing the work yourself, consider how long it would take you just to become familiar with what you're working with. What tools are needed, how is this job most easily achieved, to whom do I speak for confirmation that I'm proceeding correctly? All those issues and more must be addressed when doing any work, writing included. There is an entire professional lexicon someone new to the field has to learn before they can write a book well. That alone could account for hours lost in research, hours that you could better spend investing in your business in other ways.

Besides learning the professional language of writers, you'll also need access to resources you've only just realized exist. Not many outside the field of writing have ready access to publishers, agents, publicists, and editors. By hiring someone to ghost write for you, the process will be streamlined. You'll find yourself with a professionally published book well in advance than you might have working independently. If a ghostwriter is penning your book, you also have the added convenience of overseeing the project more objectively. With Raymond Aaron assisting, in essence you have the unique opportunity to be both the perfect storyteller and the perfect editor.

THE BUTTERFLY

by Tony Roma

My life is one dream after another, After another, into another, Over another, for another, And I dream on and on, And I CANT REMEMER THE ORIGINAL DREAM!

Is that what Catholics mean by man's original sin? Probably, maybe, hopefully... So what, who cares? But that's another dream anyway. And it only serves to understand the last, or maybe the next. But then again, or wait , I got it... Oh no, another dream.

NO MORE DREAMS! No way, that's it. Just act, right? Wrong! That's another way to dream.

Yes, schools do produce good honest fools. And even though I was born a very pensive person, Is this fleeting from idea to idea, Any more outlandish than A butterfly fluttering from flower to flower?

Written 5/2/75

Tony Roma is a dedicated businessman and family man. Extensive entrepreneurial experience paired with his education in the field of psychology has helped him create a track record of growing successful businesses. With that track record to bolster him, he now seeks to help other entrepreneurs become equally successful. According to Tony, staying on the cutting edge of marketing and branding plays a large role in achieving your business goals, and that includes authorship.

"It's not just about finding the best branding tools. It's about finding the professionals who use those tools best to help you." – Tony Roma

The Psychology of Sales

MARIBEL COLMENARES

Honestly speaking, I hate to be sold something, unless I actually want to buy it. Isn't it annoying to go into a retail shop and be followed by a sales assistant everywhere you go? It makes me feel very uncomfortable, and I imagine you have been in a similar position. Even if I am just happy looking at the products or find something I like, this behaviour normally pushes me out of a store and they miss a sale. The reason is that people do not like to be pushed into making a purchase, and pushy is what has been associated with sales for years.

Despite sales being a very honourable profession, when I first joined a sales team, selling made me feel very uncomfortable. It may sound a bit strange, but having experienced pushy sales people, I had trust issues as soon as I sensed a sales pitch. Unfortunately, I encountered poor practitioners of sales, who made me feel that they were more interested in their commissions than in helping me. When I first started selling, I had the misconception that people felt the same way about me.

I stumbled into the world of selling when I was chosen to fill a vacancy in a company providing market intelligence to the petrochemical industry through consultative sales. Thanks to the guidance of my management and teammates, as well as to the sales training provided and the sales education that I personally invested in, I managed to understand that I could be a different salesperson than those I had encountered in the past.

Through sales, I could help people unveil the pains they faced in their day-to-day activities and offer them the solutions they were searching for, but may not have realized they needed. To be a great salesperson, I needed to be a problem solver. However, I first had to uncover those problems and challenges by asking the right questions. On top of that, I learnt to listen more than I talked. I assisted my prospects or clients to understand that what I had to offer would translate into a solution for them and ultimately, benefit their company and/or their business.

Sales equals trust and respect. There have been instances where I chose to lose a sale because I knew that what I offered was not the right fit for the client. Being honest helped me to build a relationship based on truth, trust, and respect. Whenever my prospects or clients need what I provide, the chances of them coming back to me, or even recommending my services, are a lot higher.

Nobody wants to be sold, yet people want to buy. Thus, you must constantly look for ways to be personally accountable for your sales expertise and to be able to add value to the solutions that prospects, and existing clients are looking for. These will motivate individuals to continue to approach you as their trusted advisor and, at the same time, will strengthen your clients' loyalty.

WHAT DOES ADDING VALUE REALLY MEAN?

In today's global economic environment, it is not enough to have and to deliver a high-quality product or service. Adding value is a concept that many people talk about. It is believed to exist to help a business survive and thrive in such surroundings. It is all about creating a tailored customer experience based on the understanding of an individual's specific needs.

Adding value is the 'WOW' factor that determines why people decide to do business with you rather than with somebody else. It is achieved by performing daily activities and processes, whilst delivering quality at every touchpoint. Ultimately, you must enhance the experience that each customer has with your company.

A study published by Oxford University and Deloitte has been causing a lot of buzz, particularly among professionals. The study indicated that many roles in the workforce will be automated by 2030. Adding value is the best way to stand out from the competition, both virtual and human. The use of Artificial Intelligence (AI) and Machine Learning (ML), as well as the collection and exchange of data through the Internet of Things (IoT) are expected to continue to disrupt many aspects of business.

When it comes to buying, people who know what they want simply go online and buy it. So why do salespeople still exist? To add value. The next question will then be what determines who within this industry will survive? The answer would be salespeople who not only add value but continuously upgrade themselves and keep in touch with industry trends while offering their clients customized solutions. If computers and technology are constantly upgrading, shouldn't you too? Some examples of difficulties that clients face can be how to make and save time and money, improve production processes, as well as provide quick, accurate information retrieval to empower people to make key decisions. Could your products or services offer the solution to some of these common problems?

Every sales consultant needs to understand that people require inspiration to know what they want to achieve and desperation to know what they want to avoid. Clearly identifying which of these two driving forces apply to each client will enable sales practitioners to help their clients buy into a solution, either from desire, necessity or a combination of both. Moreover, it will help practitioners motivate the client into acting because they have proven that they can deliver whatever determines the client's decision.

The IoT will, in some cases, provide sales managers with behavioural data that will bring both efficiency plus a personalized experience for their clients. Marketing automation software with brilliantly personalized campaigns achieved through ML, which predicts client's behaviour from social media, provides instantaneous tailored experiences to help increase conversions and accelerate sales. When combined with smarter Customer Relationship Management systems (CRMs) it can be a valuable tool for sales practitioners to use when talking to their clients. As a result, marketing departments will be able to save thousands of dollars on irrelevant advertisements. At the same time, both marketing and sales practitioners will benefit by providing value-based solutions that understand and tackle customer needs, even before their first interaction. Thus, they can work smarter, not harder!

Regardless of whether you are a business owner, founder of a start-up or working for any company, value is a key differentiator. It will be what keeps you in business and helps you stand out from other sales people, as well as from your competitors. Do yourself, your business, your company and most importantly, your customer a big favour. LISTEN to them! Create rapport, acknowledge their needs, respect them and their time and remember details they have shared with you. If you can help them solve their difficulties, fulfil their wishes, as well as demonstrate to them that you care and that your service or product can deliver, your return on investment will be well worth your time and efforts.

UNDERSTANDING HUMAN PSYCHOLOGY

One of the biggest lies I always believed, before going into sales, was to treat others as I would like to be treated. I now know the importance of treating people as THEY like to be treated. In sales, as in any business, you need to ensure you are transmitting on the frequency of your receiver. Understanding human psychology is key to this.

It is important to comprehend that all of us have psychological motives that drive our actions. Recognizing that both motives and drives differ in strength from one person to another can be the make or break factor in closing a deal. Thus, understanding my clients, as well as the forces that motivate them to decide, is an essential skill in order to adapt my behaviour and establish a framework enabling greater and easier communication.

What would happen if people had their needs written all over them? What if there was a decoder that could help salespeople, as well as businesses, understand where their clients are coming from? For this purpose, and to be a successful sales consultant, it is important to know about the different behaviour styles decrypted in the DISC™ archetypes. This model provides a detailed analysis in terms of an individual's total self, strengths, potential limitations, fears, and the types of people they need to surround themselves with to compensate for their potential shortcomings.

Because the DISC™ model has helped me in becoming a better salesperson and in communicating more effectively, I am going to share what I believe are the most relevant aspects of it with you. Before I do so, I would like to say that in today's world, automation software is able to send prefabricated answers based on frequently asked questions, providing only general information. It lacks the personal and emotional touch. Although big data from IoT, amongst many other things, analyses behaviour, these automations are not yet able to speak in their receptors' frequency. Therefore, it is important to consider the possibility that in the near future there may exist an algorithm capable of using new metrics and user interactions to personalize conversations.

DISC™ MODEL

I would like to break down for you what DISC™ stands for:

D stands for Dominant style

I stands for Influence style

S stands for Steadiness style

C stands for Compliance style

Be aware that the DISC™ model provides stereotypical descriptions of each style. Keep in mind each person is a mix of all four styles with a tendency towards a certain type of behaviour. Remember, creating rapport is seeking first to understand, then to be understood. To be understood, you must first tailor a message that speaks to your client.

D or Dominant

Let me start by describing the "***D*** or Dominant style". People who fit into this category drive towards results, insist on immediate action to demonstrate decisiveness, like competition, tend to get impatient easily and challenge the status quo.

D style people are motivated by status, power, and prestige. They like competition, challenging themselves and they love winning. They are success driven. Thus, job descriptions and promotions are very important to them. Freedom from control and rules provide them with opportunity for individual achievement. Their goal is typically to achieve control and results, together with the autonomy to make quick decisions.

Other people with a ***D*** style share their priorities, even though they might butt heads from time to time. The characteristics that distinguish this group of people are directness, decisiveness, self-confidence, persuasiveness, as well as being problem-solvers and risk takers. Thus, different styles may find the ***D*** approach to be blunt, intimidating, or insensitive. However, it is important to understand that the reason why they act as they do, besides it being their nature, is that they fear losing, being used, or being perceived as vulnerable. Moreover, it is important to understand that stagnation, and a lack of freedom to act in order to get results, stress them.

It is also relevant to know that ***Ds*** tend to reward independence, decisiveness, straightforwardness, winning, and results. At the same time, ***Ds*** often disapprove hesitation, focus on details, and dislike oversensitivity, slowness, and weakness.

Because they have limitations, such as being impatient, perceived as insensitive, and having a lack of consideration for others, this group needs others who are patient, proceed with caution, and show consideration. They also need people who can help them calculate risks, focus on quality, and research facts.

The fast pace that continually pushes ***Ds*** forward is both their driving force and their greatest challenge. ***Ds*** can increase their effectiveness by preparing themselves to be able to provide explanations for their conclusions and changes, by being more aware of rules and guidelines, as well as by continuously receiving challenging assignments and unexpected or seemingly impossible tasks. Ultimately, they increase their effectiveness by combining their own focus and results with the team, recognizing their need for help from others, as well as how combining contributions achieves success.

Having understood the ***D*** style, it is important to be aware of how they can build a relationship with others.

For ***Ds*** to build a relationship with other ***Ds***, they will need to:

- Take the time to pay attention to the other ***Ds*** views and to recognize their opinions
- Provide other ***Ds*** the time to present their ideas without any interruptions, before they proceed to present their own thoughts
- Concentrate on an exchange of ideas instead of simply echoing each other

For ***Ds*** to build a relationship with ***Is***, they will need to:

- Discover ways to recognize ***I*** individuals, so they feel liked and valued

- Avoid pressuring ***Is*** to put success above personal relationships
- Have a disposition for small talk, before getting down to business

For ***Ds*** to build a relationship with ***Ss***, they will need to:

- Ensure a safe, friendly atmosphere, so ***S*** individuals feel at ease expressing their opinions when something troubles them
- Demonstrate concern for their emotions rather than just pressuring them to generate results
- Proactively ask for their ideas and views

For ***Ds*** to build a relationship with ***Cs***, they will need to:

- Discuss with ***C*** individuals the objective, factual aspects of ideas and assignments
- Avoid pressuring ***C*** individuals to accomplish immediate action
- Provide them with enough time to analyse their opinions

I or Influence

"*I* or influence style" approaches work with enthusiasm and enjoys collaboration and togetherness. People with this style are charming, sociable, hospitable, talkative, and outgoing. They like to encourage an environment for teamwork and relationships. Thus, they are motivated by social recognition, popularity, social acceptance, freedom from control and details, as well as the autonomy to express themselves and be inventive. They often seek opportunities to get attention, create excitement, and gain recognition, in hopes of attaining popularity, approval, and praise.

Two individuals with the ***I***-style will probably find each other's energy exciting, even if both are a little too optimistic at times (especially when it comes to time and available resources). This can result in course corrections during the work or sale process, which others can perceive as indecisiveness. Other style types may also find this sort of liveliness and fast pace to be sloppy or reckless.

Is fear social rejection, losing influence, or that someone will overlook them, their feelings, or their need for attention. ***Is*** do not like to work completely on their own, and being required to provide details, or being measured according to analysis and data, stress them out. This can cause them to lose the drive that otherwise enables them to innovate or develop ideas.

It is crucial to know that ***Is*** tend to reward creativity, enthusiasm, optimism, cooperation, and passion. At the same time, ***Is*** are prone to disapprove fixed rules, caution, a focus on details, introvertedness, and insensitivity.

Their potential limitations are that they tend to lack follow-through, be impulsive, disorganized, and overly optimistic. They often make decisions spontaneously and based on intuition instead of numbers and facts. Therefore, they need to surround themselves with people who can help them focus on the task, thus increasing their ability to follow through on completion and implementation. Someone who helps them to look for and evaluate facts, develop structures and systems, has a logical approach, demonstrates individuality, directness, as well as, sincerity will balance their characteristics.

Is can increase their effectiveness by staying focused on completing their tasks, setting priorities and meeting deadlines, approaching tasks in a structured manner, and practising strict time management. Because of their tendency to see things in a positive light, they must try to be more realistic in their praise of others, thus giving it only when it is well-deserved. ***Is*** should also be more decisive and demanding in their expectations of others. Despite their efforts to maintain a good atmosphere, they should know when there is a need for criticism and calling things as they see them.

For ***Is*** to build a relationship with ***Ds***, they will need to:

- Reduce small talk to a minimum and get straight to the point
- Be ready for ***D*** individuals' abrupt approach and not take it personally
- Share how their ideas can lead to measurable results for the ***D*** individual

For ***Is*** to build a relationship with other ***Is***, they will need to:

- Maximise the chances for cooperation and show appreciation for the other ***Is*** contribution.
- Focus on the job and at the same time be allowed to socialize
- Request other ***Is*** ideas and share their concerns

For ***Is*** to build a relationship with ***Ss***, they will need to:

- Encourage ***S*** individuals to share their views with an optimistic attitude
- Motivate ***S*** individuals to tackle difficult problems
- Ensure these individuals don't overlook problems when working as a team

For ***Is*** to build a relationship with ***Cs***, they will need to:

- Allow other ***C*** individuals to focus on the factual aspects of ideas and projects
- Not be discouraged by ***C*** individuals' reserved and sceptical attitude
- Respect these individuals' inclination for working independently

S or Steadiness

If you are dealing with someone who is an ***S*** or has a steadiness style, it is important to know that their motivations are support, sincerity, and stability. They strive to create a constant, harmonious work environment that is calm and predictable. Because they like collaboration, they often use their expertise to help and make themselves available to others. They feel happy when appreciated for their efforts, as well as for improving their team's well-being.

Saying no and putting their cards on the table can affect their ability to succeed, as well as their well-being. The reason for it is that ***S*** styles fear conflict and hate disharmony.

Because ***Ss*** love to preserve stability, changes are challenging for them, especially if those changes are sudden and unexpected. Because ***Ss*** fear readjustments, whenever a modification that affects their routine is put in place, it is better to advise them properly and in a timely manner. They also fear offending others. Therefore, ***Ss*** tend to be extremely modest with regards to their own skills. However, they are characterised as being patient, good listeners, team players, loyal, caring, reliable, and predictable.

When ***Ss*** interact with each other, they will probably appreciate one another's patience and easy-going nature, even if that means a reduced sense of urgency when working together. Other style types may see ***Ss*** as overly accommodative or indecisive.

Ss are likely to reward cooperation, loyalty, humility, thoughtfulness, and a team focus. At the same time, ***Ss*** disapprove aggressiveness, pushy behaviour, interruptions, deviations and unpredictable behaviour.

For *Ss* to thrive, they need to surround themselves with people that can collaborate flexibly, are willing to change, and can react quickly and positively to difficult problems that are unpredictable and unexpected. *Ss* also benefit significantly by working with people who can support them at prioritizing and saying no. They need others who do not have a hard time putting pressure on people, and can handle conflict more directly. This allows them to get things going and ensure tasks can be finished and delivered in a timely manner.

Ultimately, *Ss* can increase their effectiveness by being more open to changes, less modest, more confident, and being introduced to tasks and guidelines for the execution of their work.

For *Ss* to build a relationship with ***Ds***, they will need to:

- Concentrate on sharing their ideas and views early in the discussion
- Give their opinion and be direct while communicating
- Be prepared for ***Ds*** honesty

For *Ss* to build a relationship with ***Is***, they will need to:

- Maximise the chances for cooperation and show appreciation for their contribution
- Focus on the job and at the same time be able to socialize
- Request ***I*** individuals' ideas and share their concerns

For *Ss* to build a relationship with other *Ss*, they will need to:

- Give their views, making the effort to ask and listen to the other party
- Motivate each other to take on new challenges
- Ensure not to ignore potential problems when working together

For *Ss* to build a relationship with *Cs*, they will need to:

- Allow them to focus on the factual aspects of ideas and projects
- Not be discouraged by their reserved and sceptical attitude
- Respect *C* individuals' inclination for working independently

C or Compliance

When talking about people with a ***C*** style, it is important to note that they work to ensure quality and precision, and are always looking for opportunities to demonstrate their expertise. They like to have clearly defined expectations, handle tasks methodically and analytically, and to approach problems systematically and logically. This style is also known as conscientiousness.

Since high quality and accuracy are their aim, learning and skill enhancement are essential for *Cs*. Moreover, thorough analysis is needed before they can make any decision, and they tend to be very polite and diplomatic. *Cs* thrive with well-clarified expectations and standards.

The ***C*** culture is inclined to reward accuracy, completion, a focus on detail, punctuality, and reliability. At the same time, ***C*** culture tends to disapprove of mistakes, decisions based on intuition, delays, superficial research, and overexaggerated enthusiasm.

Cs fear criticism of their work, analysis, and conclusions. Mistakes, lack of time, and disorder stress them. They benefit greatly from working with people who view policies and procedures as guidelines rather than uninfringeable. They need others who think outside of the box, so that by combining their focus on quality, innovation can be created. Working with people who gets things done and are decisive is also beneficial for *Cs*.

People with a compliance style thrive in a formal work environment that provides structure and clearly communicated expectations; one that values accuracy and quality, and that praises and recognizes professional skills and results.

C style will like to work with other ***C*** styles because they prioritize getting things right. However, people with differing styles find this conscientious pace to be energy-sapping.

The ***Cs*** can increase their effectiveness by focusing on clear expectations from their task descriptions, their defined performance goals, and timelines. They can also be more effective by being more open to feedback from their peers and collaborators.

For ***Cs*** to build a relationship with ***Ds***, they will need to:

- Share the general idea without going into details
- Display their ability to work fast when the situation calls for it
- Establish parameters to work towards measurable results

For ***Cs*** to build a relationship with ***Is***, they will need to:

- Recognize that ***I*** individuals' energy and spontaneity is of value
- Avoid appearing as reserved
- Be participative in their efforts to collaborate

For ***Cs*** to build a relationship with ***Ss***, they will need to:

- Show genuine interest in ***S*** individuals' ideas and opinions in order to gain their trust

- Remember to ask more than once before they can share with you what is really disturbing them

- Avoid appearing reserved because ***S*** individuals can take this personally

For *Cs* to build a relationship with other *Cs*, they will need to:

- Focus on each other's need for facts, without trying to relate everything to logic

- Avoid misunderstandings and be willing to get to know each other well

- Respect their inclination for working independently, but be open to shared assignments

Since I have shared with you what characterises, motivates, limits, scares, and complements each style of the DISC™ model, you should now be able to start using this knowledge to create the empathy that is needed for you to convey a message in your receptors' frequency, thus increasing your sales.

Having read the different behaviour styles and motives above, you can now spot your own profile and that of your client. This will help you move on to create rapport and find your client's buying argument. After doing so, you can then motivate them into purchasing your solution by adjusting your pitch to their particular needs and style.

In the real world, it is not always that simple, because people can fit between two styles. The most important thing is to first recognize your own style(s), and get an indication of where it requires energy to adjust your behaviour to create rapport.

Start noticing where the people you work with are coming from. Whether you are simply connecting with others, solving problems, or working through conflicts, you will have to stretch from time to time in order to speak on your receiver's frequency. Remember, there is no such thing as a right or wrong profile; however, adapting to your receptor is crucial to your success.

MANAGING REJECTION THROUGH SW^4 MODEL AND IC^4 MENTALITY

Regardless whether I am dealing with business owners, CEOs, CFOs, purchasing managers, sales managers, traders, analysts, or any other market player, developing my ability to understand my client's psychology has helped me in not only closing new business, but also in managing my existing clients.

Creating rapport allows me to explore my client's needs and pains and demonstrate that the service or product I offer can deliver what they are searching for. By giving my clients information beyond the obvious, I take control of my sales questions and pitch, understand their goals and pains, manage their objections, and, ultimately, close a sale.

The "happy ending" of the sales process culminates in a closed sale, at least in an ideal world. However, in the world of sales, even top performers must face rejection. Knowing how to deal with rejection and overcoming it is a necessary skill. Ultimately, sales is a numbers game. Think of it as flipping a deck of cards, because both involve probability. Therefore, whenever I face rejection, I focus and visualize a close, and then I must keep on flipping until I get the right fit for the solution that I offer.

No one likes the feeling of being turned down, you just must keep moving ahead. Remember that every rejection brings you closer to the next "yes". At the end of the day, people could experience rejection for free and stay poor, but why would anybody do that when it could be done for money? Thus, to overcome rejection, be persistent and stay focused. You could do so by using the SW^4 Model.

SW^4 Model stands for, "Some will, some won't. So, what? Someone is waiting!"

Sharing the SW^4 Model with other sales professionals - as well as having companies implement this model - can help individuals deal with rejection and overcome the negative feelings usually associated with it. Sales professionals may be better able to stay focused, persevere and be more confident going forward, and as a result, increase chances of achieving sales targets. Understanding that tough times do not last, but tough people do, can motivate individuals to get back in the game. Once you have done the thought process for the SW^4 Model to stay focused, move forward to your visualization, which I call my IC^4 mentality.

IC^4 mentality stands for, "I couldn't, but I can! I continue until I close!"

I started sharing this mentality with my colleagues, while speaking publicly to crowds, as well as during sales trainings, with the intention to inspire people not to give up. I have found my purpose by sharing my knowledge and experiences, and it has helped others to get back in the game. When people can understand each other's minds, a different kind of intimacy, one in which you can touch lives, is created.

It does not matter if you are starting out, and have thoughts of giving up. You must always remember that every expert was once a beginner. Listen, practice, repeat; dedicate yourself to be outstanding. Remember, selling is about helping people solve their pains and problems, and creating win-win situations. Whether you have been doing this for years or you are just getting started, never stop helping people and providing value. This will open the path to becoming and remaining your clients' trusted advisor.

Closing new business is far from the end of the selling cycle. It is the beginning of finding ways to build a lifelong relationship, in which you continuously understand and exceed your client's current and changing expectations. Taking notes of those expectations and acting on them will help you safeguard your customer's satisfaction and loyalty. I truly believe that feedback is a gift, and sales professionals should take it very seriously to improve and stay ahead of the game. When doing so, opportunities for gaining clients' trust open up. Trust is the key to referrals. Ultimately, a happy customer means repeated business for life.

Achieving a Better Legacy for Private Music Students

STEPHEN RICHES

Have you reached a point in your life where you would like to try a new activity or learn a new skill? Why haven't you? If you are like many people, a few failed attempts make you believe that you aren't talented enough to master the skill set, or perhaps you believe you are too old to start. The process gets abandoned and you chalk it up to something that "wasn't meant to be."

The reality is that this does not need to happen. Becoming talented is neither a mysterious nor a daunting process, but rather, like most things in life, simply one that requires a proven successful plan of action. So right now would be a great time for you to change your perception of your own ability.

In my first book, Talent CAN Be Taught: The Book on Creating Music Ability, I debunked the myth that music talent or skill is something that only a few of the elite may enjoy, and introduced the acronym, PRAISE™, which will provide you and students everywhere with an actual blueprint for successfully developing your music skills. Even better, many of these principles may be applied in other areas of your life.

Your ability to achieve can often be wrapped up in how you view yourself. Do you see your skills as the assets that they are, or do you find yourself setting up barriers to your own success? And, with the recent discoveries by neuroscientists that point to the fact that by developing music skills you also greatly improve your brain structure and function, there may be no better way to equip yourself for a lifetime than to invest in yourself with music training.

In this chapter, I will introduce to you the principles that I have used to help my students grow music talent. Some of these, undoubtedly, will seem very logical and straightforward to you. So, if you have ever dreamed of having music talent, don't allow your fears of what others might think to stand in your way. The first step, especially if you ever had lessons in the past but gave up on your dream, is to understand that the reason most students lose interest, become discouraged and quit is because the system failed to ensure that they received the basic training that they needed to succeed.

In fact, private music lessons have presented insurmountable challenges for almost all beginning students for many decades. The problems that arise are the result of the strategies used by most music teachers and teaching studios, rather than with the students themselves, who, unfortunately, are usually blamed for their own lack of success. And, the root cause of the entire problem is one that stems from a general misunderstanding about what talent really is and how talent is created in the first place. So that is where I start my chapter.

UNDERSTANDING TALENT

Many people consider talent to be something that is innate; something that you either have or do not have, and over which you have no control. This is, in large part, due to the ideas that most of us have regarding what talent really is. If we see someone who is very young who displays music ability, we tend to say that this person is very talented. But this begs the question that if someone who is older has developed the very same skills, why should this older person not be considered to be equally talented.

In other words, why should talent simply be considered the domain of those who learn more quickly or at a younger age? Should talent not be evaluated on the basis of skills that can be demonstrated, rather than the age or the speed at which they were acquired? Just as "the proof of the pudding is in the eating", so the evidence of the talent is in the performing, rather than the age of the performer. It is these special music skills or abilities that set talented people apart and which are an indicator of their talent.

A FAILING TRADITION

Whether or not talent can be acquired is something that has been debated for many years. But where there is certainly no doubt is that in the vast majority of cases, beginning students do not become talented. And it is perhaps this fact that has led so many people to assume that their failure to progress well in developing music skills was due to an innate lack of pre-existing talent in the first place. The truth, however, is that millions of people have been victims of a failing tradition in private music education. In my book, Talent CAN Be Taught™, I first identify the signs of this systemic failure, and then present strategies that are providing exciting solutions for my students. This chapter highlights a few of the main points.

The reality is that well over 90% of all students quit private music lessons within a couple of months to a few years and go through the rest of their lives unable to perform any of the pieces that they ever learned, believing that they were responsible for their own lack of success. The causes of this high failure rate rest with critical mistakes and teaching strategies made especially by parents and teachers.

I refer to one of the causes of this failing tradition as the Tom Sawyer School of Learning, after the character in the Mark Twain novel who is able to present documented evidence of achievement without actually ever having done the required work, or acquiring the knowledge that his evidence suggests he has. First of all, he devises a strategy to get paid by his friends so that they can have the privilege of doing the work of whitewashing his aunt's fence, which she had intended to be a punishment for him skipping school the day before. And then he buys Sunday school tickets from his friends the next day by selling their loot back to them in order to receive an honour which he has not earned, in the form of an award given to all those who manage to memorize two thousand Bible verses. In the end, however, the fraud is exposed in front of the entire community, as he is unable to even correctly identify the names of just two of Jesus' disciples.

It is an unfortunate fact, however, that parents, students, and teachers sometimes work together in a way that actually defeats the system, in the same manner as Mark Twain's fictional character does. Due to a quest by parents and students to achieve accreditation as quickly as possible, teachers fail to help students to acquire any of the actual music skills that are the real purpose of the lessons in the first place. Parents and students engage in as few lessons as possible. Teachers skip pages of the curriculum books, books of curriculum levels, entire levels of curricula, and in general then "hopscotch" their way through RCM grades to acquire a Grade 7 and/or Grade 8 RCM certificate for high school credits or to pad their resumes for future career opportunities. Some students have learned as few as a couple of dozen pieces over all of their years of private music training to accomplish this feat. They do not actually learn to read music, nor do they develop the ability to play by ear, which are the two most basic of all music skills. Due to the enormous struggle involved in learning advanced level pieces with undeveloped or under-developed reading skills, even students who manage to survive hate this process so much that they abandon the music they learned forever. As a result, there is a great multitude of students who have achieved Grade 8 level of Royal Conservatory of Music certificates who are unable to play even a single piece of music that they have ever learned.

So, to summarize the problem, some of the most obvious signs of this failing tradition are:

- Inability to remember and perform any music that was ever learned
- Inability to read music at sight beyond a very elementary level, sometimes even Pre-Grade 1
- Inability to learn or play new music by ear
- Deficiencies in technical skill development
- Lack of understanding of musical style

- A more than 90% dropout rate of all beginners every three years

Compounding the problem is that many private music teachers themselves have been the product of this failing tradition. In many cases, not only do they not perform publicly themselves, but they don't even perform for their students, despite the fact that this is the most effective of all teaching strategies. Further, despite their own weaknesses, they have no plans for their own personal professional development. And so, predictably, they continue to use the same failing strategies that led to their own weaknesses and duplicate these shortcomings in their own students.

The Powerful PRAISE Techniques™ explained in detail in my first book called Talent CAN Be Taught: The Book on Creating Music Ability are the key steps which form the blueprint for successfully creating music ability. The word PRAISE is an acronym for these six very important steps to success. Following is a brief synopsis of these key steps.

THE 6 POWERFUL PRAISE TECHNIQUES™

Performance & Repertory – The Core Essence of Music

Why the system begins with performance

Music begins with performance because music is a performance art. If music isn't performed by someone, it doesn't exist. A repertory is a personal collection of music that a particular performer can play at any time by memory.

Results & Accreditation – The Benchmarks of Achievement

The value of certificates and goal setting

While seeking to acquire certificates rather than usable music skills is to put the proverbial cart before the horse, accreditation does have a valuable role to play in measuring student progress. Awards and certificates honour achievement and provide goals for the achievement of excellence. These important measurable, attainable, and most importantly, dated goals for achievement are important steps in the learning process, without which all achievement is jeopardized.

Acceleration & Motivation – The MAGIC of Synergy™

The power of this element in the learning process

One of the reasons that so many students give up on themselves is that they perceive that the learning process is taking too long and they lose interest. Most students, due to poor strategies used by their parents and teachers, never are able to develop any synergy of learning. Acquiring momentum, enjoying accelerated learning, experiencing growth of skills and abilities, feeling inspired to become even better, and being motivated by competition, (either internal or external), to achieve as high a standard of excellence as possible, are all very important steps to success for everyone in all aspects of life. Becoming musically talented is no exception.

Insights & Strategies – The Philosophy of Education

"Only perfect practice makes perfect"

Talent CAN Be Taught presents a number of important insights and strategies for the successful development of music skills. For example, it is a common misconception that practice makes perfect. Student failures, in fact, are often blamed either on a lack of talent or a lack of practice, both of which fail to recognize the real cause of the failures. This famous and often misquoted Vince Lombardi gem is one example of a philosophy or insight that is presented in the book. What the legendary football coach actually said was that "perfect practice makes perfect". However, the reality is that beginners do not know how to practice, and bad practice never achieves good results. In fact, practicing independently usually leads to frustration for almost all beginners. All students need to be first taught how to practice rather than just what to practice. And students should only be asked to practice after they have been well-prepared for independent learning. This necessarily includes having some basic reading and ear training skills. Most beginners, however, are too young to understand and use sound pedagogical strategies for independent learning. As a result, independent practice often causes more harm than good in the beginning stages of training. In the early stages, practice needs to be monitored by an expert.

Supervision & Curriculum – The Tools of Training

The role of teachers and teaching materials

Private independent teachers, by definition, have no supervisory support. Nor do many follow a curriculum in its entirety to ensure that all concepts are taught. Many or most parents either do not understand or perhaps underestimate the value or importance of the role that supervision and curriculum have to play in a student's training even though it is taken for granted in public education. The music skills that we recognize as indicators of talent do not happen by accident or over time by independent practice alone. Like all skills in all vocations, they must be taught by an expert. An important part of the TCBT system is in making sure that our teachers are equipped to provide the most expert training possible for the students. This philosophy is at the core of all that has led to the great successes of our unique Talent CAN Be Taught™ system.

The most important factor in education for all teachers and students is the need for an outstanding comprehensive and sequential curriculum. Many curricula have weaknesses in the sequence or order that concepts are taught, the size of the challenges presented to the students, and in maintaining consistently small and attainable and progressive steps for learning. These shortcomings always contribute to frustration. However, the TCBT system follows what we consider to be the very best curriculum available, which we mandate to be used by all of our teachers and students. This is also discussed in some detail in the book.

Why is using a good curriculum so important? Well, first of all, teachers are able to follow it as a daybook to systematically track the lessons that they provide. And, students who follow it are able to avoid developing gaps in their music education that always cause the learning experience to become slower, more frustrating, and less enjoyable with every level of advancement. The irony is that the shortcuts that are often taken in the quest for faster advancement and achieving higher certificates at an earlier date actually slow down the learning process. By contrast, with the TCBT system, student skill development is occurring so rapidly that some of the students have progressed from Grade 1 to Grade 6 in only two years without skipping any grade levels or exams, and have achieved First Class Honours on their exams at every level while learning hundreds of pieces of music during that time.

Ear Training & Reading Skills – The Basic Fundamentals

"Do you play by ear, or do you read music?"

As a young person, I often had an opportunity to perform for recitals or other occasions or special events. Invariably, people would see me perform by memory and ask whether I read music or played by ear. My answer, of course, was "both". At the time, I had no idea how profound this response was. For what other method is there? Either you play by ear, or you read music, and ideally both, for these are the two fundamentally basic of all music skills. And yet, both of these important skills are among the common denominators that are missing for the vast majority of students who quit taking lessons after just a few months or years. They quit because they cannot read music, nor can they play by ear, and so they find it frustrating trying to learn mainly by rote and are not enjoying it. The Talent CAN Be Taught™ system ensures that ear and reading skills are actually taught, and these vital and basic fundamentals which are taught at every step of the way complete the six Powerful PRAISE Techniques™ that contribute to the great success of the students.

The Achievers Programs™

The success of the pilot program

The Achievers Programs™ were developed to ensure student success in keeping with the principles outlined in the six Powerful PRAISE Techniques™ that make up the core part of the TCBT system. The inspiration that led to the development of these accelerated learning programs resulted from the experience of one particular student and the strategy that I implemented as a pilot program for him. This student had chosen to begin taking a trial month of guitar lessons. He could not read music, and did not know how to practice, and had become frustrated very quickly trying to practice independently six days a week. Within two weeks, he had lost interest and stopped practicing. So we made a switch. Instead of guitar, we gave him a fresh start on piano. I made a deal with him that he didn't have to practice, in order to eliminate the tension at home that had occurred due to his Mom's insistence that he had to practice every day. We gave him three half-hour lessons per week instead of one, and I reduced the price per lesson as an incentive to invest more overall to the strategy. Of course, we also used the outstanding house piano/keyboard curriculum. There were, and still are today, five main goals of this program as follows:

- provide more frequent, regular, expert teacher support
- reduce per-lesson cost to encourage parents to make a larger short-term financial commitment
- enhance foundational learning with a switch to piano training
- eliminate the source of tension and liabilities associated with forced independent practice
- to create synergy among the various learning components with the frequency of instruction

Less than three months after starting this pilot program, I discovered that the student, who had been working with another teacher at my studio, was beginning the fifth level in the curriculum. And this curriculum had 4 books at each level. His mother had this explanation for how he had managed to go through 16 curriculum books in just 10 weeks:

"Oh, I forgot to tell you. He won't stop practicing. He practices at all hours during the day, even first thing in the morning before school. I put an alarm clock on the piano set for 8:15 AM. I tell him that when the alarm goes off, he has to stop playing the piano and go to school, or he is going to be late. I may be upstairs vacuuming and hear the alarm go off. I turn off the vacuum cleaner to listen, and the sounds from the piano keep on going. So I have to come downstairs to physically remove him from the piano bench and send him off to school."

So what happened here? Well, this student, who had previously very quickly become disinterested in the instrument of his choice (guitar), was now thriving on piano as a result of the implementation of the Powerful PRAISE Techniques™ that form the core principles of the TCBT system. I immediately began to promote these strategies for all of our students. Within three years, all of the students who participated in the program were able to accelerate through as many as eight levels of study achieving excellence at every level.

BUILDING A NEW LEGACY FOR THE FUTURE

An Innovative Teacher Apprentice Program

The best of systems can only reach its ultimate achievement when it is duplicated. That, of course is the principle behind the great successes of franchising. And just as many teachers are duplicating their own weaknesses in their students and thereby contributing to the continuation of the failing traditions, so the TCBT teacher apprentice program has been designed to continue and duplicate a new and better system of private music education. This program is designed especially for high school age students who have achieved RCM First Class Honours in Grade 5 Piano and Basic Theory. Students who have not yet achieved this standard of excellence, but who are currently studying at this level may also be admitted to the program. In the apprentice program, students are provided with an opportunity to first improve the quality of their own learning through examination of teaching practices and study of curriculum materials, to earn community service credits for high school by assisting beginning students, and eventually to earn part-time income through teaching beginning level students themselves. Those who progress to the highest levels of achievement will have an opportunity to become leaders of the Talent CAN Be Taught™ system to continue the legacy for future generations.

While piano/keyboard training is the best foundation for all music studies, the principles, of course, are transferable to other instruments and voice. At TCBT studios, we encourage many students to diversify and take a second instrument when they are ready for the additional experience. Some may receive this supplemental training in the public education system, but many do not. And all benefit greatly from receiving supplemental expert support with their band or orchestra instrument that isn't available in the context of a music classroom setting. Without exception, these students become the leaders in their school music programs.

AN AFTERWORD TO THE CHAPTER

In Talent CAN Be Taught; The Book on Creating Music Ability, I drew attention to the shortcuts that students were taking, and the resulting mine field that causes almost all private music students to get frustrated and give up on themselves within a few months to a few years. They incorrectly assumed, or in some cases were perhaps even told that the reason that they were not progressing was because they lacked talent, when, in fact, the real reason was due to historically ineffective teaching routines and strategies, and especially the ill-advised shortcuts that have been used by parents, teachers, and students for many years. These are explained in detail in the book, along with numerous recommended solutions.

In this single chapter, therefore, I have merely summarized and highlighted some of the key points of the book, while necessarily leaving out an explanation of most of the important details.

So while I hope that you found this chapter helpful as an introduction to the topic of how to ensure quality results with private music lessons, I encourage anyone who is serious about developing music skills to read the entire book.

In summary, the book includes a detailed explanation of many of the most common errors made by parents, students, and private teachers engaged in private music education. It also includes a diagnostic survey that will help readers to recognize if they have been a victim themselves of what I refer to as the failing traditions. Finally, it provides the proven blueprint for success through a detailed explanation of the role of The Powerful PRAISE Techniques™, as well as a number of helpful insights and strategies for success. These are critically important for all students of any age who would like to have great music skills, even for those who had previously given up on their own personal quest for talent, and who may now be inspired to renew their efforts buoyed by a better understanding of the proven keys to success.

TESTIMONIALS

"Stephen's vision and commitment to achieving a better future for private music education is truly inspiring. His passion for excellence, which I have been privileged to observe firsthand, is evident in his book's reflections and challenge for future engagement."

Reg Andrews
Administrator, Pickering Christian Academy, (Markham, ON)
www.pca.ca

"If your child is now or soon will be taking piano lessons, you need to read this book, because all students deserve to have teachers who really understand and value the important lessons this book contains."

Frank Feather
global business futurist, author, and father to two pianist daughters (Aurora, ON)
www.ffeather.com

"I took piano lessons for 9 years as a child and today, I cannot play anything! I thought that was because I was not naturally talented. If I had understood the concepts in this book – that talent can be taught – today I would be a professional piano player, entertaining people around the world!"

Dr. Robert A. Rohm Ph.D
speaker, author (Atlanta, GA)
www.personalityinsights.com

"I first met Stephen around the time he published his first book. I was so impressed with his commitment to making changes to improve how music is taught for the benefit of students everywhere that I invited him to be co-author of my second volume of *The Road to Success*"

Jack Canfield
entrepreneur, success coach, and co-author of the
Chicken Soup for the Soul books (Santa Barbara, CA)
www.jackcanfield.com

Bringing Balance to Your Life

DENNIS GARRIDO

When I woke up in the hospital staring up into the terrified eyes of someone I cared about, after my second cardiac arrest in one year, I knew that things had to change in my life. Especially because I was only in my twenties at the time.

Everything in my life was out of balance. Obviously, physically because I was lying in the emergency room, but more importantly my mind, emotions, and spirit were completely out of whack, and that had taken a toll on my body.

Now you may be wondering how someone so young could have had two cardiac arrests before the age of 30? It won't be hard to imagine once I share my story with you. I wish I could tell you that I had a great upbringing, one filled with laughter and love, but it wasn't.

At age eleven I was removed from my parent's home by The Children's Aid Society because they deemed my parents unfit to raise me. During that time, I went through a whirlwind of emotions. A part of me was happy that change was finally occurring, because clearly at that point, the way things were, wasn't working at all.

Another part of me felt fear because of the unknown. I didn't know exactly where I would be living, nor did I know for sure what my group & foster homes would be like, what the other kids would be like, what the living conditions would be like, how far or close I'd be to my family and hometown, etc. Essentially, I wasn't 100% certain nor 100% convinced that I was going into better circumstances.

Also, I felt sad, since I wouldn't see my parents or siblings anymore, nor my home town and many of the people whom I'd see on a regular basis; everything FAMILIAR would be gone! Lastly, I felt angry, that it had come to me being removed from my parent's house, away from those who were in my life for all those years. As twisted and messed up as it may be, I was angry that I was leaving a life that I had become accustomed to and felt somewhat comfortable in (comfortable in comparison to the unknown that lay ahead); and most of all, angry that I was leaving FAMILIARITY!!!!

Please understand me, I am no longer angry at my parents, and you shouldn't be either. They did the best they could, but when you are broken yourself, unless you find a way out, you will repeat what had been bestowed on you from the previous generations. I can be thankful because what I went through helped create the person I am today and as a coach, it gives me great empathy and understanding to be able to help others. So, don't feel sorry for me because even though my life had a rough start, I get to choose the rest of it and it is going to be GREAT!!!

THE NEXT SEVEN YEARS OF MY LIFE

For the next seven years until I turned 18, I was bounced from foster/group home to foster/group home. I rarely spent more than three months at any one place, and it caused some major emotional setbacks that took me a long time to overcome.

One of the biggest negative emotional setbacks was again to do with familiarity. As I spent time with those at my new home, seeing them every day and coming to know them personally; I naturally formed a connection/friendship with them. It seemed that no sooner had I done that; they were removed from my life. People whom I really liked (a few of them, whom I loved), ALL GONE!!! Which basically solidified my already ingrained defence mechanism of keeping distant from others; not allowing anyone to get close enough to form any connection with me.

Inevitably, this made it very difficult for me to form any type of relationship with anyone. School and extracurricular activities were hard because I never knew how long I would be staying in one place. What was the point of making friends if I could never keep them? It was a lot easier to keep my distance than to reach out yet again and have everything torn away from me.

Eventually, I started to tear down the wall that prevented me from getting too close to anyone. To this day, the negative emotional setbacks I experienced, still affect me to some degree; though I CHOOSE not to allow them to prevent me from forming meaningful relationships!

THE DARKEST TIME OF MY LIFE

All that change led to one of the darkest periods of my life. Emotionally and mentally I had shut down and could no longer function. Life was so hard. Even things that were simple, now became agonizingly difficult and it hit the point where I didn't want to live anymore. What was the use of carrying on in this horrible life when there wasn't any hope of it changing?

My life began to narrow down to one permanent solution, and that was to end it all by committing suicide. I just couldn't handle life anymore, but I truly believe that Almighty God, the universe or whatever you want to call it, had a bigger plan for me. Even though I tried several times, I just couldn't die!!! Because of those attempts, I ended up in psychiatric institutions, a few times.

It finally came to the point where I was tired of trying to die, I was tired of institutions and I was weary from all the self-harm, and so I came to a decision. I guess you could say that it was a turning point in my life; I wasn't going to attempt suicide anymore. I wasn't sure what to do because my circumstances hadn't changed, but I was willing to look for options. That was the beginning point of change in my life. The will to live!!!

IT DIDN'T GET BETTER RIGHT AWAY

Life is a journey with twists, hills, and valleys of varying shapes and sizes, with occasional points where you make decisions that put you on a different path. The determination not to kill myself had set me on a new road, but I still didn't know what to do or which way to go. It was slow going as I fumbled my way through, but at least I was moving forward!!!

At age 18 I was no longer in the custody of The Children's Aid Society, so, I moved back with my parents, which was the perfect testing grounds for me to apply the life lessons I had learned so far. You would be amazed by how much maturity one can have at 18 when you have been through what I have. It wasn't easy, and it was hard work, but I managed to re-establish a relationship with my parents and not only complete high school, but also graduate from post-secondary schooling.

One of the things I had decided to do was get my student loans paid off in the six-month grace period, which I managed to do; but in doing so, I pushed myself way beyond my physical limits which brought on the first cardiac arrest.

You would think I would have learned from that first experience, but I didn't, and less than a year later we are back to the beginning of this chapter waking up in the hospital from my second one.

This time I learned my lesson and chose a different path, but I still didn't know how to achieve what I needed. For so long I had lived in imbalance, that I didn't know where to start, but the catalyst for change was just around the corner.

I FINALLY REALIZED WHAT BALANCE WAS

Believe it or not, it is the simplest things that can bring about the most profound changes in life. My search for balance in my life had begun, and it is amazing how the answer came; by a knock at my door one day.

That day I was busy working on something, so when the first knock came, I ignored it. It was only after a couple of rings of the doorbell that I finally decided that I would answer it. There was a well-dressed gentleman at the door and even though I don't remember most of what he said, one thing became clear, I was missing an essential element to finding the balance I craved. Now, I knew what it was. You can only find balance when you address ALL the areas of your life, and I had been missing one. The spiritual side.

It is amazing what happens when you finally have all the pieces together. As I started to study the Bible, I finally could build a solid spiritual foundation, that enabled me to re-evaluate things in my life, and thus, put a plan together to create balance in my life. In the rest of this chapter, I am going to share with you what I learned.

Just before I do that, I do want to mention one thing. All of this is a process. Can I say that I am 100% balanced in my life? No, but when I started at 3-4% and then jumped to 85%, I think that is very good growth. It's difficult to attain 100% balance in every aspect of one's life, that is why even the most successful people keep learning and growing. So, the goal is not perfection, but growth. As long as you are continuing to move forward, that is all that matters.

7 STEPS TO BRING BALANCE TO YOUR LIFE

Here's one of the things that I have learned about bringing balance to your life. In some ways, it is easy. The steps I am going to teach you are simple to understand. The hard part is training yourself to be aware of it every day and live by it. The good thing is, though it may be hard at first, the more you practice it, the easier it gets.

STEP 1

Ask yourself, "What are my priorities in life?" You want to look at it from all aspects of your life, personal and professional. In terms of personal that includes goals physically, emotionally, mentally, spiritually, relationships (such as your spouse or significant other), family and friends. You want to look at it from the point of what you need and what you want. For each one, you should have one to two priorities.

In terms of professional, they can include your current work situation and areas of improvement there, plus plan for your future. Put down both needs and wants.

	NEEDS	WANTS
PERSONAL		
PROFESSIONAL		

STEP 2

Look at your needs column. What are the most important priorities personally and professionally? It is important that you only start out working on a few at a time. If you try to do everything at once, you will become overwhelmed and quit. Then, figure out the things you need to do to get those needs met.

STEP 3

Now go through your wants and do the same thing as Step 2 above. Don't overlook this. Part of having balance in life is having both your needs and wants met. Obviously, your needs are more important, but without the wants, you give up hope.

STEP 4

Set up a timeline for those needs to be accomplished. What are you going to do today, this week, this month, this year, and in the next five years to bring yourself to reach those priorities?

STEP 5

Do the same thing for your wants. Set up your timeline of completion.

STEP 6

DO THE ACTIONS. Here is where the rubber meets the road. You can plan and plan and plan, but if there is no action involved you will be in the same place, with the same problems, five years from now.

STEP 7

Re-evaluate. Every few months go back through this whole process again.

As you grow and change, so will your priorities, your needs and your wants.

THE BEST WAY TO ACCOMPLISH THIS

Very rarely can a person accomplish this alone. Have you ever heard the saying, "You can't see the forest for the trees?" That is what happens in our lives. We get so caught up in the unimportant things right in front of us, that we miss the big picture and we don't recognize growth when it occurs.

Now, you do have several options. One is to have family members try to help you through this. While you do need their support, they are usually looking at the same trees you are and can miss things.

Two, you can go to friends for help. They do tend to see more of the big picture, but many times they can't give you the encouragement and motivation you need at times to get past yourself.

Three, you work with a professional who knows how to help you bring balance to your life. They can come alongside of you and guide you to the quickest path to success because there will be obstacles that try to stop you. Did I forget to mention that?

No road to balance is smooth; little pebbles will get into your shoes to irritate you and take your focus off your goals. Barriers will be put up that you will have to learn how to go over, under, around or through. People will get in your way and tell you that it is the wrong road to take and you should follow them. All sorts of things will try to keep you from what you want.

Coaches are keen observers who can not only help you with what is going on right now, but they have been down your road and they know what is up ahead and can keep you moving forward, even when everything is telling you to stop.

That is what I'm offering to be for you. Let me help you on your path to balance in your life. I have been on both sides of the coin, and I can guide you through the roughest parts. I can relate to what you are feeling and am more than willing to help you navigate this wonderful thing called life.

First of all, if you would like more information on how to start this process, you can pre-order my upcoming book at www.dennisgarrido.com Second, you can email me at dennis@dennisgarrido.com and request your free 15-minute phone consultation where we can discuss your situation and see if we are a good fit for each other. Third, maybe you realize more people need to hear this message. I am also available to speak to groups and conferences. If so, just send me an email, and we can arrange a time to speak.

No matter what you decide, know this. You can achieve balance in your life. It is possible. I can tell you that it has been worth everything I went through to get to this point. The peace I experience now, compared to the chaos I lived before, is so amazing and I wish the same for you.

Don't miss out. Make the choice to change your life today, and I guarantee that you won't regret it!!!

www.ingramcontent.com/pod-product-compliance
Lightning Source LLC
Chambersburg PA
CBHW052005090426
42741CB00008B/1553

* 9 7 8 1 7 7 2 7 7 2 3 6 4 *